Sustainable Development

SUSTAINABLE DEVELOPMENT

Kumar Das
Senior Professor
Department of Applied Economics,
Utkal University
Bhubaneswar

Reference Press
4831/24, Ansari Road, Darya Ganj,
New Delhi-110002
Tel. : 23260807, 41563444
Fax : 011-41563334
E-mail: info@essessreference.com
www.essessreference.com

Reference Press
4831/24, Ansari Road,
Darya Ganj,
New Delhi-110 002.

Tel.: 23260807, 41563444
Fax: 41563334
E-mail: info@essessreference.com
www.essessreference.com

Rs.625/-

First Published - 2009

ISBN: 978-81-8405-045-5

Cover Design by Patch Creative Unit

Published By Reference Press and printed at Salasar Imaging Systems

PRINTED IN INDIA

In the loving memory
of
My Mother
Tara Devi

Contents

Preface

Certainly the idea of sustainable development has become increasingly popular in the contemporary world. Sustainable development has become a buzzword, being used in too many contexts today. We hear about sustainable development, sustainable growth, sustainable economies, sustainable societies, sustainable agriculture sustainable livelihood. Everything is sustainable. New books on sustainable development have been appearing with increasing rapidity since Earth Summit, 1992. According to Brundtland Commission it is the development that "meets the needs of the present without compromising the ability of future generations to meet their own needs." The field of sustainable development is conceptually divided into four general dimensions: social, economic, environmental and institutional. The first three dimensions address key principles of sustainability, while the final dimension addresses key institutional policy and capacity issues.

Sustainable development is an eclectic concept, as a wide array of views fall under its umbrella. Different conceptions also reveal a strong tension between ecocentrism and anthropocentrism. Thus sustainability is a process which ensures the development of all aspects of human life .It means resolving the conflict between the various competing goals, and involves the simultaneous pursuit of economic prosperity, environmental quality and social equity famously known as triple bottom line with the technological vector. Hence it is a continually evolving process. Thus sustainable developemnt process is that trajectory which is the synergy of efficiency, equity and sustainability.

Globalisation has created an atmosphere of excitement of instant economic growth. It is based on invisible hand and focuses on the free marketism.neconomic theory mainly relies on There is sharper obsession for economic development to be achieved by laissez faire policy . Whole world is moving ahead with the pragmatism of high tech and excitement of achieving higher economic efficiency. Western society has become materialistic, consumption-oriented, and spiritually barren. These are all direct consequences of the Newtonian paradigm. There is sharper obsession for economic development, which is logically based on the pragmatism of Darwinian principle of efficiency.

Man extracts inputs from the environment and produces outputs. The first one refers to the depletion of natural resources and the second one refers to problems of environmental degradation. Environmental Economics studies the trade off between a set of social choices: higher economic quantity and higher environmental quality. Both the objectives are conflictual to each other. Healthy economy creates unsound environment and healthy environment results in inefficient economy. An "unsustainable situation" occurs when natural capital is used up faster than it can be regenerated. Sustainability requires that human activity only uses nature's resources at a rate at which they can be replenished naturally. The sustainable development debate is basedon the assumption that societies need to manage three types of capital (economic, social, and natural), which may be non-substitutable and whose consumption might be irreversible.

Sustainable Development has become a matter of policy debate. There are a number of important antecedents to the report by the United Nation's Brundtland Commission (1987). United nations devised the Agenda 21, related to sustainable development. The Summit also adopted treaties and 27 principles on climate change and biodiversity. These principles, though very general, are especially significant since they represent a series of difficult-to-reach compromises between industrialized and developing countries. The Rio principles includes: a state's sovereign right to exploit its own resources in accordance with its own policies, without harming the environment elsewhere .Thus, sustainable development, as a policy concept, has two main pillars: economic development and the consumptive use of the world's natural resources in ways that are sustainable. It emphasizes on both efficiency and intergenerational equity with intragenerational equity. We do not have to choose between an environmentally healthy and economically robust nation. We can have both. The whole idea of sustainable development needs serious revision. Sustainable development does not focus solely on environmental issues either. We are intelligent enough, have the ability to develop enough new technologies, and can change our behavior enough to confront all the problems facing us and create the optimal solutions.

Sustainable development is said to set limits on the developing world. While current first world countries polluted significantly during their development, the same countries encourage developing countries to reduce pollution, which sometimes impedes growth. It serves as a pretext for developed countries for the protectionism. Sustainable development has a legion of practical problems There is a now a world wide movement of environmentalism parallel to the global movement of economic growth.. Every section of people around the globe now express some amount of concern towards the deterioration of environmental standards. Some group of environmentalist are very pessimistic while the other group of environmental scientists are very optimistic. But the fact remains that every section of people around the globe now express some amount of concern towards the deterioration of environmental standards. There is acid raining, global warming, greenhouse effect, erosion and sterility of soil, degradation of land, environmental pollution ,ozone layer depletion and instability in the ecosystem. . The rise in economic welfare is increasingly accompanied by a considerable decline in the quality of environment and loss of ecological stability.

This book is the outcome of my presentations in several national conferences and international seminars. It also contains revised versions of some of my research papers published in reputed international journals. It also includes my lectures delivered at different professional fora. Later on I observed the convergence of my ideas and common line of my thought in seminars presentations. I am thankful to the organizers of those seminars and editors of different journals who have permitted me to published these materials in the form of this book. I express my deep sense of gratitude to my friends and colleagues of Asian University, Bangkok Sanghai University, Hongkong university who have encouraged me to bring out this book. Particularly I am thankful to Dr P. Temie, Dr Peter Gruberman, Dr. Suthiporn, Dr. Peter Nijkamp, Dr A. Amin for their useful comments on the earlier draft of the manuscripts. My thanks are also due to my students and research scholars for whom my ideas and lectures have constantly got refined. I am thankful to my better half, my younger brother, Nira, Nirmala, my sons, Leonard, Maynard and Nikhil and for their loving support during the preparation of this manuscript. I thank Mukesh Graphics for completing the DTP job very neatly and Mr. Sumit Sethi, the publisher for bringing out the book in time.

Kumar Das

1
Introduction

Sustainable development has become a buzzword in different fora, seminars , workshops and found in much environmental and some economics literature these days. The word sustainable comes to us from the foresters of the 18th and 19th century in Europe. At the time much of Europe was being deforested, and the foresters became increasingly concerned since wood was one of the driving forces in the European economy. Certainly the idea of sustainable development has become increasingly popular in the contemporary world. The word sustainable has been used in too many situations today, and ecological sustainability is one of those terms that confuse a lot of people.We hear about sustainable development, sustainable growth, sustainable economies, sustainable societies, sustainable agriculture. Everything is sustainable.[1] New books on sustainable development have been appearing with increasing rapidity since the United Nations Conference on Environment and Development (the Earth Summit) held in Rio de Janeiro, Brazil in June of 1992, and the number of articles appearing in professional journals has been expanding at an exponential rate. World Summit on Sustainable Development took place in Johannesburg, South Africa, from 26 August to 4 September 2002. Then what is sustainable development anyway? And more importantly, why does sustainable development matter?

The term, "Sustainable development" was coined by the Brundtland Commission which defines sustainable development as development that "meets the needs of the present without compromising the ability of future generations to meet their own needs." [2] It means "living standards that go beyond the basic minimum are sustainable only if consumption standards everywhere have regard for long-term sustainability" [3] Sustainable development is defined as balancing the fulfillment of human needs with the protection of the natural environment so that these needs can be met not only in the present, but in the indefinite future. Sustainable development is a pattern of resource use that aims to meet human needs while preserving the environment . The field of sustainable development is conceptually divided into four general dimensions: social, economic, environmental and institutional. The first three dimensions address key principles of sustainability, while the final dimension addresses key institutional policy and capacity issues.

Thus sustainability is a process which ensures the development of all aspects of human life affecting sustenance. It means resolving the conflict between the various competing goals, and involves the simultaneous pursuit of economic prosperity, environmental quality and social equity famously known as three dimensions (triple bottom line) with is the resultant vector being technology. Hence it is a continually evolving process. The 'journey' (the process of achieving sustainability) is of course vitally important, but only as a means of getting to the destination (the desired future state). However,the 'destination' of sustainability is not a fixed place in the normal sense that we understand destination. Instead, it is a set of wishful characteristics of a future society.

Sustainable development is an eclectic concept, as a wide array of views fall under its umbrella. Different conceptions also reveal a strong tension between ecocentrism and anthropocentrism. TSustainable development ties together concern for the carrying capacity of natural systems with the social challenges facing humanity. As early as the 1970s "sustainability" was employed to describe an economy "in equilibrium with basic ecological support systems" [4]. Ecologists have pointed to the "limits of growth"[5] and presented the alternative of a "steady state economy"[6] in order to address environmental concerns. The field of sustainable development can be conceptually broken into three constituent parts: environmental sustainability, economic sustainability and sociopolitical sustainability. The along side figure-1 illustrates the three dimensions of sustainable development. Sustainable development can not ignore any of the three. If we ignore the social dimension, the development process may be viable, if we ignore the environmental dimension, the development process may be equitable and if we ignore the environmental dimension, the development process may be bearable, but not sustainable. In otherwords the search for equity(a) neglects environmental aspects, and the search for viability(b) neglects social dimension and search for bearability(c) ignores economic effciency. Thus sustainable developemnt process is that trajectory which is the synergy of efficiency, equity and acceptability.

1.1. HISTORY OF SUSTAINABLE DEVELOPMENT

During 18th and 19th century much of Europe was being deforested, and the foresters became increasingly concerned since wood was one of the driving forces in the European economy. Forests were best harvested from an economic standpoint using clear-cutting techniques. But

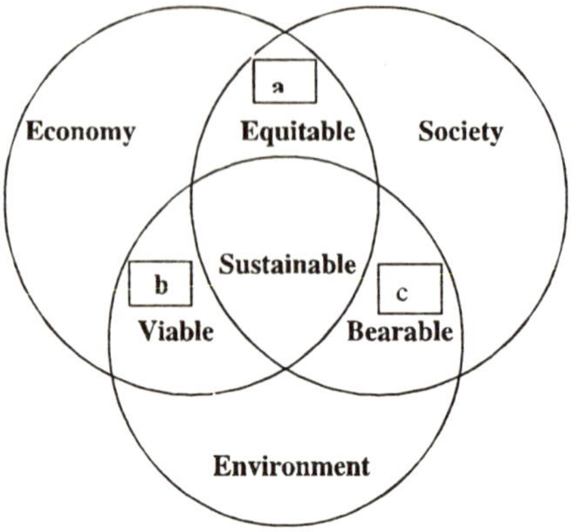

Fig. 1.1 : Sustainable Development

the forests that grew back after clear-cutting did not always provide the wood needed for the European economy. If enough trees were planted to replace the wood that were harvested every year, then the forest would be sustainable. Thus, in this original idea, sustainable means that as a resource is used, it is replaced by growing additional amounts of the resource. In the modern context of the word, sustainable, this is a difficult context because there are many resources, such as oil or iron ore, that cannot be grown. Still, these resources, like the trees in Europe's forests, are finite. If all the oil is extracted, there will not be any more oil. Still, if humanity is to survive with a civilization for another 1,000 years, we are still going to need to heat our homes and fulfill many of the same purposes that oil now fulfills.

The word development, at least as it is used in the phrase sustainable development, has a different history. During the cold war the United States needed to respond to the Communist challenge in the Third World that said that communism would bring with it a new standard of living. Walt Rostow, a prominent economist, developed a competing ideology that he called economic development. Under the Communist model societies that staged a revolution against the proletariat and threw off the shackles of capitalism would begin a transformation that would lead to economic equality between all people. All of the wealth of a nation could then be used to raise the standard of living and well-being of all the people within that society. The attractiveness of this model to the poor people of the Third World is obvious. It promised masses of people a significantly better way of life.

Rostow's answer to this challenge was that it was the task of civilized world to economically develop the Third World. Rostow, and then the U.S. government and the governments of Western Europe and Japan, believed that all the civilized world had to do was to prime the economic pump of capitalism in the Third World, and just like a real pump, when enough dollars were inserted into an economy, the Third World economy would take off. This would eventually result in a better standard of living, a developed rather than a developing society, and a world safe for democracy and capitalism. Thus, according to this model, the poor would be much better off in the long run by embracing democracy and capitalism. If the Third World country would remain anti-communist, they would receive foreign aid , at some point in the future, take off and become equal to the economies of Western Europe, the U.S. and Japan and other advanced countries. It leads to convergence of economies.

1.2. ECONOMIC DEVELOPMENT

The mainstream of Economics is confined to the analysis of logical choices and purely instrumental allocations of given scarce resources to given competing ends. The traditional neoclassical economic theory mainly relies on invisible hand and focuses on market transactions. The scope of this conventional analysis is inadequate for obtaining insight into the interwoven and interdependent environmental problems, which fall frequently outside the realm of market transactions. But since Economics is particularly concerned with the conundrum of scarcity, it is obvious that environmental quality analysis benefits by the use of economic theory and logic.

There is a now a world wide movement of environmentalism parallel to the more enthusiastic global movement of economic growth. There is sharper obsession for economic development to be achieved by laissez faire policy of free market mechanism. Whole world is moving ahead with the pragmatism of high tech and excitement of achieving higher economic efficiency. On the contrary every section of people around the globe now express some amount of concern towards the deterioration of environmental standards. The rise in economic welfare is increasingly accompanied by a considerable decline in the quality of environment and loss of ecological stability. Some group of environmentalist are very pessimistic while the other group of environmental scientists are very optimistic. But the fact remains that there is acid raining, global warming, greenhouse effect, erosion and sterility of soil, degradation of land, environmental pollution and ozone layer depletion. There is wide spread desertification in one hemisphere and deforestation in another hemisphere of the globe. Deeper and wider concern for environmental degradation springs from two major sources:

(1) Rise in material production and use of synthetic materials and rise in quantity of effluents, have led to considerable decline in the environmental quality or services.

(2) Increased demand for environmental goods, which in turn codetermined by the increased scarcity of environmental goods

The first one refers to the problems of environmental externality and the second one refers to depletion of natural resources. In addition to the increased supply of pollutants, there is also an increased demand for environmental goods. Environmental goods connotes any external environmental conditions and influences that affect human welfare. These conditions and influences may have different characteristics. The following elements are connected with the human environment

- Absence of all types of pollution
- Availability of cleaner water and air
- Quality of natural environment(outdoor recreation etc)
- Quantity of natural environment(forest, wildlife)
- Availability of public utility systems
- Average space availability by inhabitants

These elements, inter alia, belong to the area of Environmental economics. The increased scarcity of environmental goods implies that economics can act as a very useful discipline in order to solve these problems involving the finiteness of natural resources.

Traditional economics is hardly concerned with analyzing the tradeoffs between increases in the capital stocks and production on the one hand and the associated social cost on the other hand. Environmental Economics studies the trade off between a set of social choices. Both the objectives are conflictual to each other. Healthy economy implies unsound environment and Healthy environment implies inefficient economy. Higher GNP implies larger quantity of goods and services, which ultimately results in larger quantity of byproducts and polluting materials .It results in environmental loading, which are detrimental to the environmental soundness.

1.3. ENVIRONMENTAL SUSTAINABILITY

Environmental sustainability is the process of making

sure current processes of interaction with the environment are pursued with the idea of keeping the environment as pristine as naturally possible based on ideal-seeking behavior. An "unsustainable situation" occurs when natural capital (the sum total of nature's resources) is used up faster than it can be replenished. Sustainability requires that human activity only uses nature's resources at a rate at which they can be replenished naturally. Inherently the concept of sustainable development is intertwined with the concept of carrying capacity. Theoretically, the long-term result of environmental degradation is the inability to sustain human life. Such degradation on a global scale could imply extinction for humanity.

Consumption of renewable resources	**State of environment**	**Sustainability**
More than nature's ability to replenish	Environmental degradation	Not sustainable
Equal to nature's ability to replenish	Environmental equilibriumeconomy	Steady-state
Less than nature's ability to replenish	Environmental renewal	Sustainable development

The sustainable development debate is basedon the assumption that societies need to manage three types of capital (economic, social, and natural), which may be non-substitutable and whose consumption might be irreversible. Daly for example, points to the fact that natural capital can not necessarily be substituted by economic capital. While it is possible that we can find ways to replace some natural resources, it is much more unlikely that they will ever be able to replace eco-system services, such as the protection provided by the ozone layer, or the climate stabilizing function of the Amazonian forest. In fact natural capital, social capital and economic capital are often complementarities. A further obstacle to substitutability lies also in the multi-functionality of many natural resources. Forests, for example, do not only provide the raw material for paper (which can be substituted quite easily), but they also maintain biodiversity, regulate water flow, and absorb CO2. Another problem of natural and social capital deterioration lies in their partial irreversibility. The loss in biodiversity, for example, is often definite. The same can be true for cultural diversity. For example with globalisation advancing quickly the number of indigenous languages is dropping at alarming rates. Moreover, the depletion of natural and social capital may have non-linear consequences. Consumption of natural and social capital may have no observable impact until a certain threshold is reached. A lake can, for example, absorb nutrients for a long time while actually increasing its productivity. However, once a certain level of algae is reached lack of oxygen causes the lake's ecosystem to break down all of a sudden.

1.4. MARKET FAILURE

If the degradation of natural and social capital has such important consequence the question arises why action is not taken more systematically to alleviate it. Cohen and Winn (2007)point to four types of market failure as possible explanations: Firstly, while the benefits of natural or social capital depletion can usually be privatized the costs are often externalized (i.e. they are born not by the party responsible but by society in general). Secondly,they add that many times natural capital is also undervalued by society since we are not fully aware of the real cost caused by the depletion of natural capital. Information asymmetry is a third reason identified to cause natural and social capital depletion. Often the link between cause and effect is obscured, thus making it difficult for actors to make informed choices. Cohen and Winn close with the realization that contrary to economic theory many firms are not perfect optimizers. They postulate that firms often do not optimize resource allocation because they are caught in a business as usual mentality.

The most broadly accepted criterion for corporate sustainability constitutes a firm's efficient use of natural capital. This eco-efficiency is usually calculated as the economic value added by a firm in relation to its aggregated ecological impact. This idea has been popularised by the World Business Council for Sustainable Development (WBCSD) under the following definition: "Eco-efficiency is achieved by the delivery of competitively-priced goods and services that satisfy human needs and bring quality of life, while progressively reducing ecological impacts and resource intensity throughout the life-cycle to a level at least in line with the earth's carrying capacity." (DeSimone and Popoff, 1997: 47)

Similar to the eco-efficiency concept but so far less explored is the second criterion for corporate sustainability. Socio-efficiency describes the relation between a firm's value added and its social impact. Whereas, it can be assumed that most corporate impacts on the environment are negative (apart from rare exceptions such as the planting of trees) this is not true for social impacts. These can be either positive (e.g. corporate giving, creation of employment) or negative (e.g. work accidents, mobbing of employees, human rights abuses). Depending on the type of impact socio-efficiency thus either tries to minimize negative social impacts (i.e. accidents per value added) or maximise positive social impacts (i.e. donations per value added) in relation to the value added.

Both eco-efficiency and socio-efficiency are concerned primarily with increasing economic sustainability. In this process they instrumentalize both natural and social capital aiming to benefit from win-win situations. However, as Dyllick and Hockerts point out the business case alone will not be sufficient to realise sustainable development. They point towards eco-effectiveness, socio-effectiveness, sufficiency, and eco-equity as four criteria that need to be met if sustianable development is to be reached.

1.5. POLICY CONCERNS

Sustainable Development has become a matter of policy debate. There are a number of important antecedents to the report by the United Nation's Brundtland Commission (1987). Our Common Future marks the beginning of the sustainable development concept that has generated all the literature and recent commentary. Divergent economic theorists like E.F. Schumaker of Britain, environmentalists like Barry Commoner and Lester R. Brown, population analysts like Paul Ehrlich, politicians like Willy Brandt of what was then West Germany and Jimmy Carter of the United States, discussions within the United Nations and United Nations agencies, and a number of environmental organizations spread throughout the world all played significant roles in formulating ideas that became part of the Brundtland Commission's message. But even though many of the concepts of sustainable development existed before 'Our Common Future'. Brundtland report started the process of making sustainable development an important policy issue. United nations devised the Agenda 21 .It is a programme run by the United Nations (UN) related to sustainable development. It is a comprehensive blueprint of action to be taken globally, nationally and locally by organizations in every area in which humans impact on the environment.

The Commission identified a number of "common challenges" facing the earth: Population and human resources, food security, species and ecosystems, energy, industrial development, and urbanization. In the context of these challenges they discussed international environmental problems, what successes had been registered in trying to address those problems, the scope and nature of the environmental problems still facing the world community, and the role of the world's economic systems in developing solutions to these problems and providing long-term relief for what they perceived to be the related problems of poverty and underdevelopment.

Thus, sustainable development, as a policy concept, has two main pillars: economic development and the consumptive use of the world's natural resources in ways that are sustainable. We have to consume, in other words, with the realization that resources are finite. Our job as human beings is to preserve the human future on this planet into a limitless future. It involves "equity and the common interest." It emphasizes on both efficiency and intergenerational equity with intragenerational equity. According to Brundtland Commission, the "ecological interactions do not respect the boundaries of individual ownership and political jurisdiction." Nor has the local nature of human interaction with the environment been confined to local environmental effects. Rapid growth in production has extended production to the international plane, with both political and economic manifestations. To the Commission "the enforcement of common interest often suffers because areas of political jurisdiction and areas of impact do not coincide". In addition, the Commission continues, there is currently an inequitable distribution in resource consumption:

The search for common interest would be less difficult if all development and environment problems had solutions that would leave everyone better off. This is seldom the case, and there are usually winners and losers. 'Losers' in the environmental/development conflicts include those who suffer more than their fair share of the health, property, and ecosystem damage costs of pollution .This inequitable distribution is of increasing concern . Because, as a system approaches ecological limits, inequalities sharpen and hence, our inability to promote the common interest in sustainable development is often a product of the relative neglect of economic and social justice within and amongst nations. [7] In other words the winners in the battle to consume from the earth's many commons create a dilemma for those who recognize the need for sustainable use since efforts to preserve the commons' various assets, as the system approaches ecological limits, increases both economic and social injustice within and amongst nations.

1.6. RESPONSES TO OUR COMMON FUTURE

There are two responses of sustainable development initiative. One approach calls for continued economic growth with the growth made more environmentally sensitive "in order to raise living standard globally and break the link between poverty and environmental degradation," and the other calls for radical changes in the world's economic order.[8] One example of the reactions of those calling for economic growth with environmental responsibility is the report, "Choosing a Sustainable Future," released by the National Commission on the Environment. The report begins with a warning that "if America continues down its current path, primarily reacting to environmental injuries and trying the repair them, the quality of our environment will continue to deteriorate, and eventually our economy will decline as well." The report's message is: "If, however, our country pioneers new technologies, shifts its policies, makes bold economic changes, and embraces a new ethic of environmentally responsible behavior, it is far more likely that the coming years will bring a higher quality of life, a healthier environment, and a more vibrant economy for all Americans"[9]

In other words, if we keep our heads, recognize the seriousness of the environmental crisis, and then act boldly to meet the various challenges of that crisis, we can not only turn around the quality of the environment, but we can keep a vibrant economy as well. We do not have to choose between an environmentally healthy and economically robust nation. We can have both. We are intelligent enough, have the ability to develop enough new technologies, and can change our behaviors enough to confront all the problems facing us and create the optimal solutions.

A more radical approach to sustainable development was published by Lester W. Milbrath in a book entitled Envisioning a Sustainable Society, released only two years after publication of Our Common Future. Calling for: an end to the idea of a growth economy, an end to the culture that always accepts scientific advancement as a positive good, and the beginning of a society that learns its way to an infrastructure designed for sustainability, among other proposals, Professor Milbrath asserts that "Anyone who calls for a massive transformation of society is bound to be an impractical dreamer. I am calling for people to transform the most basic of all relationships, their relationship to nature. The changes I have proposed will surely be difficult to adopt. Yet, modern society's only choice is to change." [10] The idea of sustainable development is more idealistic, rather than practical. Modern society's only choice is to "change" is repeated over and over again in all the literature. We are in trouble, and something positive must be done.

1.7. THE EARTH SUMMIT

After, and in the midst of the literary ferment arising from the Brundtland Commission report, including some powerful, deep ecology work by poets and essayists like

Wendell Berry and Gary Snyder and novelists and essayists like Edward Abbey, the Earth Summit was proposed and planned by the United Nations. The United Nations Conference on Environment and Development (UNCED) was held during June 3-14 in 1992 in Rio de Janeiro, Brazil. One hundred and fifty nations sent representatives, 1,400 non-governmental organizations were in attendance, 8,000 journalists covered the event.

The major accomplishments of UNCED centered around task of furthering the work of creating sustainable development policies and procedures throughout the world. Other bodies were created out of "conventions" passed at the Summit on climate change and biodiversity. These particular organizations are to be dedicated to developing scientific and technical advice related to the development and implementation of international treaties. The basic ideas are that treaties entered into by the world's nations should, in the future, make sure that treaty provisions do not contribute to climate changes that have the potential to harm life on the planet earth and should help protect the planet's biodiversity. The Planet Earth Council and the Business Council for Sustainable Development were also created as the result of the Summit.

The Summit also adopted treaties on climate change and biodiversity .But the treaty on biodiversity was resisted by the United States government until Bill Clinton became President. The Summit also adopted the Rio Declaration that includes 27 principles. These principles, though very general, are especially significant since they represent a series of difficult-to-reach compromises between industrialized and developing countries. Much of the developing world feels that the industrialized countries have used up the world's environmental resources in their pursuit of development and now wish to protect what environmental resources are remaining at the expense of the possibility of economically improving the lot of poor nations. These principles, then, provide a framework for the world's diplomats in their efforts to improve both environmental and economic conditions around the world. The Rio principles included: a state's sovereign right to exploit its own resources in accordance with its own policies, without harming the environment elsewhere (principle 2); the right to development (principle 3); environmental protection as an integral part of development (principle 4); sustainable development that requires reducing 'unsustainable patterns of production and consumption' and that promotes 'appropriate demographic policies' (principle 8); access to information and citizen participation (principle 10). . .and the polluter pays principles, including the internalization of costs and the use of economic instruments (principle 16)[11] After the Earth Summit the literature and discussions about sustainable development exploded. Newspapers, business magazines, science journals and magazines, popular magazines, television, radio, and a host of other forums and conferences centered on a discussion of sustainable development. In some parts of the world, such as in New Zealand, sustainable resource management concepts designed to improve the environment while, at the same time, helping New Zealand meet economic goals, were adopted into new legislation. [12] The first stirrings of a national sustainable development policy in the United States were also felt when President Bill Clinton declared in December of 1992 that "our future depends on maintaining a sustainable environment, and in so doing we can create economic opportunity".[13]

1.8. THE SKEPTICISM

Sustainable development is said to set limits on the developing world. While current first world countries polluted significantly during their development, the same countries encourage developing countries to reduce pollution, which sometimes impedes growth. Some consider that the implementation of sustainable development would mean a reversion to pre-modern lifestyles.There are those, of course, who question the whole sustainable development concept. Stephen R. Dovers and John W. Handmer, writing in Environmental Conservation, discovered what they described as eight "obvious" contradictions in the new movement. According to them within each there exist many levels and tensions.[14] At the heart of the Dovers and Handmer criticism is a sense that the sustainable development discussion to date has been more rhetoric than an honest attempt to deal with facts and numbers. They admit that humans can live with logical inconsistencies and still work toward solutions, but overall they are pessimistic in that ". . .our numbers, per *caput* consumption, and total load on the Biosphere, continue to increase." They are afraid that the contradictions they see in the sustainable development movement "are perhaps insurmountable in any morally-defensible way," and that "the magnitude of the problems of environment and development can be overwhelming enough, let alone when matched with the magnitude of the cultural and political obstacles to change" inherent in the concept of sustainable development. In other words, they are afraid the contradictions within the various ideas that make up sustainable development as a concept are both too profound and insurmountable to overcome .[15] Stanley Temple of the University of Wisconsin questions the very use of the phrase, sustainable development. It confuses a lot of people. The result of the overuse of the word, sustainable, in Temple's view, is that it has come to mean too much and nothing at the same time. Therefore sustainable development as a concept is too largely drawn to have any particular usefulness. The major point to be derived from reading the literature critical of the idea of sustainable development is that this is a movement that is more ethereal than concrete. There are a lot of discussions about the pending doom of biosphere if the environment is not protected more vigorously and efficiently than in the past in the pro-sustainable development literature. There is a call for economic and resource equity between the peoples currently living on the earth and between living generations and unborn generations. But, as the critics are pointing out, there is a lot of fuzziness that does not make the concept of sustainable development concrete. The word sustainable, as Temple points out, has become a buzz word that is used to the point of distraction. What does it really mean? Does it mean that resources must be protected at all cost? Should they be protected to the seventh generation? Or should resources be protected forever? And which resources should be protected? Are we really going to try to live without oil or a whole host of useful mineral resources? What, exactly, does sustainable mean in the context of sustainable development?

Equally difficult questions can be raised about the word, development, in the sustainable development context. The Brundtland Commission appears in Our Common Future to want to primarily improve the economies of the Third World so that the living standards of those living in countries mired in poverty can be raised to a more acceptable level. Development in Europe, Japan, the United States, and in places like Korea, Taiwan, Thailand, and other rising economies, has a much different meaning. Neo-classical economists like Milton Friedman believe passionately that the free market demands that all people in all places at all times have the right to improve their economic well being. In his book, Free to Choose, written with his wife Rose Friedman, he asserts that the two ideas of human freedom and economic freedom working together came to their greatest fruition in the United States. Those ideas are still very much with us. We are all of us imbued with them. They are part of the very fabric of our being. But we have been straying from them. We have been forgetting the basic truth that the greatest threat to human freedom is the concentration of power, whether in the hands of government or anyone else. [16] We have persuaded ourselves that is safe to grant power, provided it is for good purposes. Fortunately, we are waking up. We are again recognizing the dangers of an overgoverned society, coming to understand that good objectives can be perverted by bad means, that reliance on the freedom of people to control their own lives in accordance with their own values is the surest way to achieve the full potential of a great society. [17]

Are the great societies ready to limit their consumption, their pursuit of economic and human freedom, in order to guarantee equity between either current populations or future generations if that is a necessary pre-requisite of achieving the ideal of sustainable development? Can the idea of economic freedom be maintained in a sustainable developed society? A society that can sustain its use of natural resources and the environment forever? Or is the whole idea of sustainable development a buzz-word pipe dream conjured up by idealists who fail to realize that the world and humankind are realities?

The work of the idealists like Milbrath(1989) is both entertaining and a dead end road. The entertainment value derives from the power of speculations about the future. But in the end fiction, although it may give insights into realities, cannot resolve the conflicts and contradictions that are part of both the human and the earth's condition. No blueprint of Shang-gri-la will bring Shang-gri-la into existence. No road map to Shang-gri-la will lead to the creation of paradise. is to The task of those who believe that the idea of sustainable development is more than a pleasant fiction construct a model of sustainable development based upon the characteristics of an observable model, even if the model is incomplete in that it is not as fully sustainable or as fully developed as the proponents of the sustainable development concept would desire. The value of such a model is that it can be used to eliminate some of the fuzziness surrounding the idea of sustainable development and can also be used to encourage policies and practices that can, really, lead to a more sustainable developed world.

John Baden(2007) reckons that the notion of sustainable development is dangerous because the consequences are proceedings with unknown effects or potentially dangerous. He writes: "In economy like in ecology, the interdependence rules applies. Isolated actions are impossible. A policy which is not enough carefully thought will carry along various perverse and adverse effects for the ecology as much as for the economy. Many suggestions to save our environment and to promote a model of 'sustainable development' risk indeed leading to reverse effects." Jean-Marc Jancovici (2002) criticises the terma as too vague. Luc Ferry(2007)says that the term "sustainaible development is obligatory, but absurd, or rather so vague that it says nothing." Luc Ferry adds that the term is trivial by a proof by contradiction: "who would like to be a proponent of an "untenable development! The term is more charming than meaningful. According to Sylvie Brunel(2008), the ideas of sustainable development can hide a will of protectionism from the developed country to impede the development of the other countries because it serves as a pretext for the protectionism. She says, "I have the feeling about sustainable development that it is perfectly helping out the capitalism" The proponents of the de-growth reckons that the term of sustainable development is an oxymoron. According to them, on a planet where 20% of the population consumes 80% of the natural resources, a sustainable development cannot be possible for this 20% : "According to the origin of the concept of sustainable development , a development which meets the needs of the present without compromising the ability of future generations to meet their own needs, the right term for the developed countries should be a sustainable de-growth"

To sum up, this is only the lightest introduction to the idea of sustainable development and the controversies surrounding the idea. Sustainable development has a legion of practical problems that stand between the world today and its eventual realization. To those that believe the free market is the answer to all of the world's problems, sustainable development is a dangerous notion that can bring the prosperity of the U.S., Western Europe, and Japan crashing into a prolonged economic dark age. To environmentalists who are worried about concepts like the carrying capacity of the earth and the long-term needs of human survival, sustainable development is a shining promise that must be reached if the world is saved. For those in poor countries who are desperate for a more equitable distribution of wealth, it is an idea with enormous appeal. There is a now a world wide movement of environmentalism parallel to the global movement of economic growth. There is sharper obsession for economic development .Whole world is moving ahead with the pragmatism of high tech and excitement of achieving higher economic efficiency. On the contrary every section of people around the globe now express some amount of concern towards the deterioration of environmental standards. The rise in economic welfare is increasingly accompanied by a considerable decline in the quality of environment and loss of ecological stability. Some group of environmentalist are very pessimistic while the other group of environmental scientists are very optimistic. But the fact remains that there is acid raining, global warming, greenhouse effect, erosion and sterility of soil, degradation of land, environmental pollution ,ozone layer depletion and instability in the ecosystem. .

The whole idea of sustainable development needs serious revision. Sustainable development does not focus solely on environmental issues. It includes the notions of weak sustainability, strong sustainability and deep ecology. The United Nations 2005 World Summit refers to the "interdependent and mutually reinforcing pillars" of sustainable development as economic development, social development, and environmental protection. Agenda 21 clearly identified information, integration, and participation as key building blocks to help countries achieve development that recognises these interdependent pillars. It emphasises that in sustainable development everyone is a user and provider of information. It stresses the need to change from old sector-centred ways of doing business to new approaches that involve cross-sectoral co-ordination and the integration of environmental and social concerns into all development processes. Furthermore, Agenda 21 of UN emphasises that broad public participation in decision making is a fundamental prerequisite for achieving sustainable development. Thus sustainable development is not same as green development. Green development is generally differentiated from sustainable development in that Green development prioritizes what its proponents consider to be environmental sustainability over economic and cultural considerations. Proponents of Sustainable Development argue that it provides a context in which to improve overall sustainability where cutting edge Green development is unattainable.

REFERENCES

1. Temple, Stanley, interview remarks, "Old Issue, New Urgency?" *Wisconsin Environmental Dimension*, Spring 1992, Vol. 1, No. 1, p. 1.
2. United Nations. 1987."Report of the World Commission on Environment and Development." General Assembly Resolution 42/187, 11 December 1987. Retrieved: 2007-04-12
3. WCED(World Commission on Environment and Development), Our Common Future Oxford, England: Oxford University Press,1988, p. 44.
4. Stivers, R. 1976. The Sustainable Society: Ethics and Economic Growth. Philadelphia: Westminster Press.
5. Meadows, D., Meadows, D. L., Randers, J., & Behrens, W. 1971. The Limits to Growth. New York: Universe Books.
6. Daly, H. E. 1973. Towards a Steady State Economy. San Francisco: Freeman. Daly, H. E. 1991. Steady-State Economics (2nd ed.). Washington, D.C.: Island Press.
7. WCED, 1988, op cit, p. 49.
8. Carley, Michael and Christie, Ian, Managing Sustainable Development, Minneapolis: University of Minnesota Press, 1993. p. 42
9. National Commission on the Environment, Choosing a Sustainable Future," (Washington DC: Island Press,1993, p. xi.
10. Milbrath, Lester, W., Envisioning a Sustainable Society, Learning Our Way Out New York: State University of New York Press, 1989, p. 352
11. Haas, Peter M.; Levy, Marc A.; Parson, Edward A., "The Earth Summit, How Should We Judge UNCED's Success?" *Environment*, Vol. 34, No. 8, October 1992, p. 12
12. Robertson, James, Future Wealth, A New Economics for the 21st Century New York: The Bootstrap Press, 1993.
13. Appenzeller, Tim, "Environment and the Economy," *Science*, Vol. 260, June 1993, p. 1883.
14. Dovers, Stephen R. and Handmer, John W., "Contradictions in Sustainability," *Environmental Conservation*, Vol. 20., No. 3, 1993, p. 217(Dovers and
15. Ibid, p. 221.
16. Friedman, Milton and Friedman, Rose, Free To Choose New York, Avon Books, 1979.
17. Ibid, p. 297.

2
Environmentalism and Developmetalism

Developmentalism and Environmentalism are inherently conflictual. Strong agreement regarding their compatibility has emerged conceptually but large gap has remained practically. It is a great challenge. Accepting the challenge involves substantial distortions and costs, but failing to face the challenge is more disastrous. This chapter argues to integrate the economy, environment and society by an ecosystem approach which is only practicable in a decentralised framework. Ecosystem approach can ensure intergenerational equity.

Man's obsession with economic development is termed as developmentalism. Around the globe, throughout the history most modern human institutions have evolved in ways that are at best oblivious of and at worst positively hostile to the nature. The process of development, regardless of the economic system, commit two types of fallacies (1) It treats environment as a commodity; and (2) it considers the humanity and ignores the interdependent system.

The concern for environmental crisis is termed as environmentalism. It is the time when everyone on the planet claims to be environmentally conscious and expresses at least some level of concern about nature's health. There are extra ordinary divergent views about the real connotation of environmentalism. Some view it in religious sense in reverential tone and advocate for true natural world. Some view it in humanist perspectives and advocate for modification and intervention to accommodate the needs of humanity as perfectly as possible, accommodating other species only to the extent that meets the human requirement. Some view it in terms of intergenerational equity. Some argue to protect the biodiversity of nature down to the level of insects. Environmentalism in developing and third world countries is not a phenomenon of post materialism. It is not a post-industrialisation luxury of the first world. It is a more complicated phenomenon emerging from multiple sources and complex forces like (a) Environmental justice and social protests (b) Mass media diffusion of environmental values (c) direct observation of environmental degradation (d) institutional processes and (e) transnational urban culture.

2.1. ENERGY AND ENVIRONMENT

Energy plays that role in an economy, which 'food' plays in the biological system of a living being. It is the backbone of every nation and lifeblood of every economic activity. Ultimately energy is the means and not the end. The use of energy has a two-fold linkage effect with the Economy.

(i) The increase in energy consumption necessarily effects a proportional increase in productivity or performance and ensures a steady economic development.

(ii) The cost of energy consumption necessarily puts a

burden on the Economy and affects its overall performance.

The relationship between environment and economic development has never been happy one. Development has often harmed the environment and the environmental harm has in turn adversely affected development. There is a close nexus between energy consumption pattern, environmental standards and ecological problems of the world. One of the major crisis, the world is facing, is that of heavy deforestation. From environmental point of view it is a real disaster. Forest performs irreplaceable ecological services and provides economic products and other facilities. It assists in global cycling of water, oxygen, carbon and nitrogen. It maintains stability in hydrological systems. Thus the formulation of an energy policy is a key element in maintaining and improving the environment, because the pattern of energy use affects the environment is an almost infinite number of ways[1]. Environmental problems refer broadly to the negative influences of human activities on natural environment beyond the sustainable level. There are three types of negative influences[2] material extractions, environmental disturbance by artifacts and other man-made activities and chemical-physical pollution. These distinctive influences can be linked to various types of natural resources (renewable and non- renewable) and assimilative capacity.

Most important example of common property resource is the waste assimilative capacity of the environment. Environmental externalities are inherent and pervasive consequences of the extraction, processing, consumption and discharge of physical materials and energy. The relationship between energy flow and the environment is shown in fig.2.1. In a fixed environment, growth of material consumption leads to corresponding increase in waste flows. If there is no environmental assimilation the density of cumulative pollution inevitably rises.

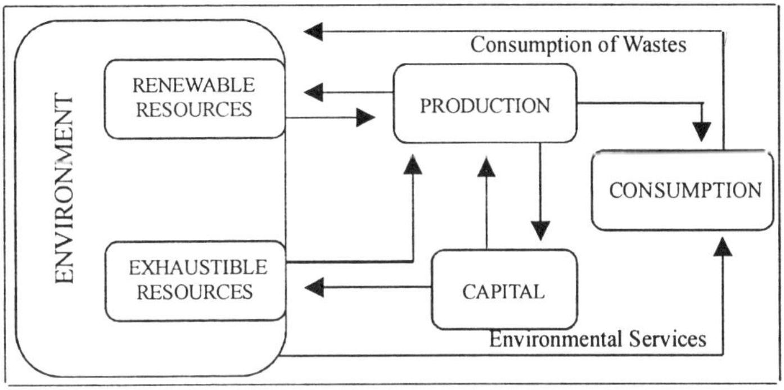

Fig. 2.1: Energy and Environment

Firewood crisis is always localised in its apparent dimensions. The accelerating degradation of woodlands throughout Asia, Africa, Latin America caused by fuel gathering lies at the heart of profound challenges to environmental stability, severe soil erosion, menacing floods, creeping deserts and declining soil fertility and land productivity. The fossil fuel emissions of principal concerns include sulfur dioxide, nitrogen oxide, carbon mono and dioxide, various hydrocarbons, fly ash and suspended particulates. They attack human health, damaging body tissue and the nervous systems, bringing increased respiratory diseases and cancer, causing higher morbidity and mortality in sensitive segments of populations. Transformed into acid, they burn and spoil vegetation, corrode buildings and vehicles and eventually pollute water, air and land. Coal combustion necessarily produces carbon dioxide. Adding CO_2 to the air raises earth's temperature[3]. Therefore, development of new technologies to solve environmental problems is going to be a major task over the next few decades, which provides the real test of man's wisdom. In particular, the spotlight is going to fall on the relationship between energy and the environment.

2.2. DOOMSDAY SCENARIO:

The matter used to be taken for granted has now become an issue of great concern for the entire world. The global energy crisis with all its manifestations is largely the result of the myopic vision of the world's past and present political and economic leadership[4]. But Economists frequently tend to dismiss the doomsday scenario of depletion and pollution with cheerful platitudes. GNP rightly subtracts the depreciation of plants and equipments from overall output of goods and services. But it takes no account of the depreciation of natural capital, such as loss of topsoil from erosion, the destruction of forests by acid rain, or depletion of the protective stratosphere ozone layer. As a result the economic accounting system greatly overstates the progress of human civilisation. Failing to reflect the reality it generates environmentally destructive economic policies[5]. On the contrary the biological accounting system is almost non-existent and fragmentary. It does not warn us when the carrying capacity thresholds are crossed. The result of this flawed economic accounting and largely non-existent biological accounting is widespread degradation and destruction of the life support system. An expanding economy based on such an incomplete and defective accounting system is expected to slowly undermine itself and eventually collapse.

The finitude of the earth and its resources set the limit to economic growth of both developed and developing countries. The earth does not and can not supply us with an unlimited amount of usable energy, raw materials, foodstuffs, safe dumping grounds for the waste products or even standing room. It is not an inexhaustible cornucopia.

2.3. ENERGY STARVATION

Rural Energy crisis of India is different from that of

developed countries. It is very complex in its origin and manifestation. Energy problem of advanced countries relates to energy-inefficient methods or the energy-uses which do not significantly enhance people's wellbeing or quality of life[6]. But for most of the developing countries, the existing energy situation is more one of debilitating inadequate nutrition, virtually a condition of energy starvation. The structure and functioning of rural fuel economy in developing countries is quite different. There is a clear dividing line between the pattern of energy consumption of the poor and non-poor. Fuel procurement and use and the mechanism by which people cope with energy shortage and depletion radically differ. Cash fuel economy of the modern sector functions above the horizontal line and subsistence fuel economy of the rural sector functions below it. (Fig-2.2). There is two-fold division of energy use in the subsistence fuel economy. There is very little or no scope for energy-use in the service sector. But in the cash fuel economy, there is a three-fold division of energy use domestic sector, productive sector and service sector.

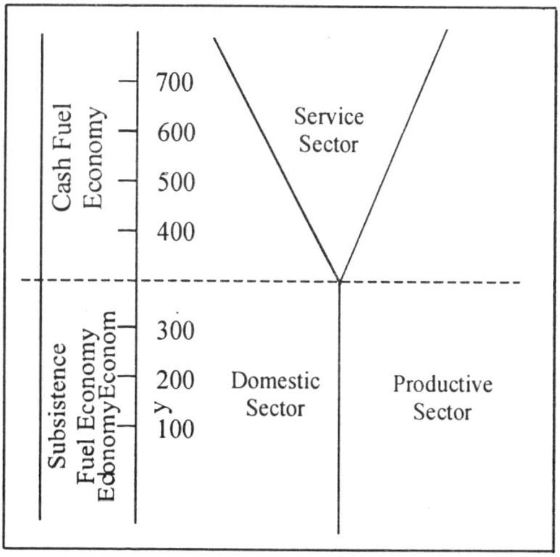

Fig. 2.2 : Rural Fuel Economy

The rural poor of all developing countries mostly depend on the non-commercial energy sources. The household expenditure of 80% of rural population is abysmally so low that it is unlikely to purchase anything else other than food. The rural majority are too poor to enter into the market of commercial energy. Therefore, they have no option other than surviving on non-commercial energy sources firewood dungcake and agricultural wastes etc[7]. The characteristics of non-commercial energy is that it is there for 'gathering' and is available at zero private cost for the villagers. Thus the significant majority of rural population living below or just above the poverty line has not yet crossed the 'fuel-gathering' stage. The worry about the cooking fuel is the most common problem for rural people. Fuel cost is rapidly rising, more so in the villages. It is tending to exceed the cost of food it is to cook. It is not what is in the pot, but what is under it, that worries the poor villagers[8]. So cooking fuel in the Indian villages have always been limited to the energy sources available from the immediate environment. As a result firewood is now being consumed more rapidly than it is being regrown. It results in a vicious circle, which necessitate each family to devote more of its time and labour for searching ever farther away from its home for fuel wood. As the forests are badly damaged and eliminated entirely, vast areas of topsoil are left exposed to rain, wind and floods. Erosion of topsoil not only contributes to the silting of water ways and eventual flooding downstreams, but also accelerates the loss of productivity of land, on which the villagers survive. This effect is further exacerbated by the increasing tendency to burn animal dungs, which is formerly served as a vital soil fertiliser. Thus the depletion of traditional fuel energy and non-affordability of the commercial alternatives worsen tthe energy-starvation of the poor villagers and simultaneously undermine their capability to produce food for their own subsistence.

The rate of growth of consumption of commercial energy in India has increased by 4.52% during 1980-90. The percentage share of agricultural sector in energy consumption has increased up to 7.55% during the same period. The elasticity of energy consumption in India during different period have been estimated (table 1). Elasticity of energy consumption with reference to coal and oil has declined to 1.12 and 1.57 respectively.

This indicates that there is substitution of others forms of energy in India.

Table 2.1 : Elasticity of Energy Consumption in India

Period	*Rate of growth of commercial energy consumption*	*% share of agriculture in energy consumption*	*ELASTICITY OF ENERGY CONSUMPTION*			
			Coal	*Oil*	*Electricity*	*Total commercial energy*
1953-60	5.47	1.75	1.10	2.14	3.02	1.37
60-70	4.29	2.80	0.53	2.31	3.04	1.16
70-80	4.21	4.95	0.98	1.83	2.00	1.37
80-90	4.52	7.55	0.31	1.12	1.57	0.8

2.4. SUSTAINABLE DEVELOPMENT

One does not know if life exists elsewhere in the universe. We are the only life that exists. In such a situation, preserving life in this planet and improving the human conditions must be the goal of development. We must seek for building a "steady-state society[9]. It is that society which is dedicated to living with environmental constraints rather than perpetually growing with the hope-less goal of conquering nature.[10] The emerging questions of international concern like, global acidification, climatic change, global warming, deforestation and ozone depletion are increasingly looked at from the view point of sustainable development. The notion of sustainable development can be regarded as the result of the need to solve a potential and/or actual conflict between developmentalism and environmentalism, with a particular view on efficiency and equity, now and in the future[11]. It recognises the goal of the survival of human species, of the realisation of an acceptable quality of life for each individual in present and future generations[12], and of a wise management of natural resources and ecosystems, with the help of a broader economic system.[13]

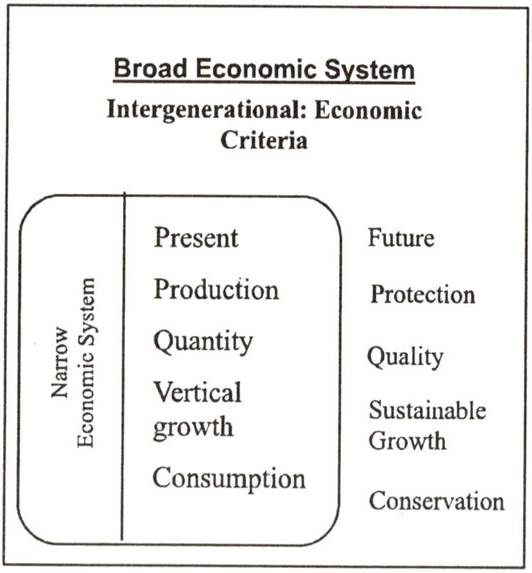

Sustainable development integrates the imperatives of developmentalism and environmentalism. It highlights the long term doomsday scenario and puts emphasis; on economic - ecological integration and regional scale. It consists of all the objectives, (Efficiency, growth, more production, more consumption, more quantity, etc.) of narrow economic system. Ecological sustainability also requires economic efficiency.[14] But an efficient use of resources need not be a sustainable one. It shows a compassionate concern for the posterity and for the world as a whole. It contends that environment and economic growth are not contradictory or incompatible. Healthy

Environment and sound resource base are rather prerequisites for sustainable development which is defined as the progress that seeks to meet the needs and aspirations of the present without compromising the ability of future generations to meet their requirements[15]. This reconciles the need for conservation with the need for development at on stroke. Sustainable Development is based on a broader economic system which fulfils inter-generational equity criteria. Its objectives are future quality, protection, conservation etc. The environmental and natural resources directly affect the standard of living or quality of life of people. The welfare of the individual is ultimately dependent upon the viability of life supporting system. An apparently efficient development path may not be sustainable.

Sustainable development reconciles the need for environmental conservation and developmental thrust at one stroke. It is based upon a broader economic system, which includes all activities that affect the environment and energy base. An analysis of the capability of the economic system for resolving economic problems of allocating scarce resources to different and competing ends must include both the flow of natural and environmental resources into the production process and the flow of wastes from the production and consumption activities back to the environment.

Figure 2.3 illustrates the broader economic system. Both the environmental services and resources directly affect the quality of life of people. Welfare of the society ultimately depends upon the life support system[16].

Sustainability necessitates the maintenance of the level of well-being so that it improves, but at least never allows a decline through time. Trends continued can not be simply assumed. The implications for valuation is quite different, necessarily more stringent than what is implied by consideration of efficiency alone. The broad economic system should emphasise on green growth and green GNP.

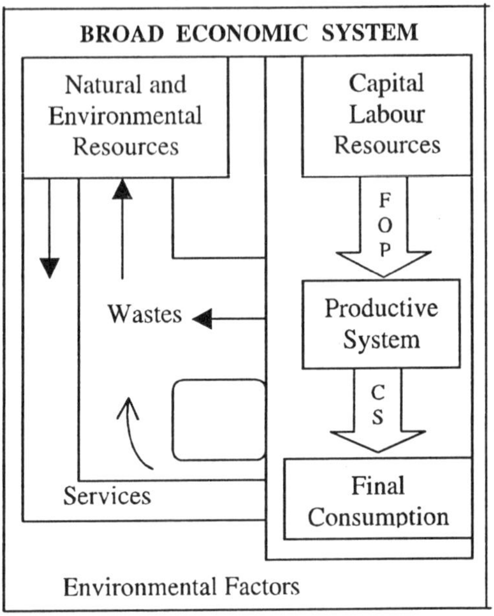

Fig 2.3 : Broad Economic System

Economic development adversely affects the environment, which undermines the health and reduces the quality of life. It eventually slows down the process of economic development. On the contrary sustainable development improves and conserves the environment, which encourages the development process. Development with sound environment and ecological balance improves the health and quality of life which eventually maintains the sustainable development.

2.5. SUSTAINABILITY IN AGRICULTURAL DEVELOPMENT

Economic growth is undermining the carrying capacity of the earth leading to the tragedy of commons.[17] Land is becoming less fertile and forest is being destroyed.

Reduction in the carrying capacity is taking place at an unprecedented rate today around the third world such as over planting, over-cutting of forests over fishing, over haunting, over grazing, over pumping and over production of waste and effluents all leading to environmental deterioration and ecological imbalance. The agriculture on which large majority of rural population of the third world eke out their living, directly depends on natural ecosystems and resources. It is most vulnerable to environmental degradation, which along with emerging agro-climatic constraints is slowing down the agricultural production and world economic growth.[18]

The major goal of sustainable Agricultural development (SAD) in developing countries like India is to create and maintain secured livelihood options for the rural people.[19] An indicator for sustainable development should reflect all the three dimensions i.e. economics, ecology and intra and inter genrational equity. Here an attempt is made to measure the sustainable livelihood security (SLS) index[20] and to empirically illustrate its practical utility and policy relevance. Sustainable livelihood security is defined as the livelihood level which is economically efficient, ecologically secure and socially equitable.

The SLS Index is a generalised relative approach underlying the Human Development Index developed by UNDP in 1990. It is measured here by the formula:

$$Z_{ijk} = \frac{S_{ijk} - Min\, S_{ijk}}{Max\, S_{ijk} - Min\, S_{ijk}} \quad \text{(for positive indicator) (1)}$$

$$Z_{ijk} = \frac{Max_{ijk} S_{ijk} - S_{ijk}}{Max\, S_{ijk} - Min\, S_{ijk}} \quad \text{(for negative indicator) (2)}$$

Where: (i =1,2........ n), (j =1,2 ....m), (k =1,2........ s)

Where: Z_{ik} = SLS index of *i*th region in terms of *j*th component and *k*th variable

S_{ik} = Value of *i*th region, in terms of *j*th component and *k*th variable.

The numerators in the above formula measures the extent by which *i*th region did better or worse in *k*th variable representing *j*th component of SLS Index as compared to the region having the worst or best performance. The denominator is the range of a given variable across regions. Having calculated the Z_{iji} for all the variables, the indices for the various components of SLS are calculated as a simple mean of the indices of their respective variables. That is:

$$Z_{ij} = \left[\frac{\sum_{k=1}^{s} Z_{ij}}{s} \right] \quad (i = 1,2 \ldots.n)$$

$$(j = 1,2 \ldots.m) \qquad (3)$$

Then the composite indicator for each region is estimated as a weighted mean of the component indices obtained from equation (3). That is:

$$Z_{ij} = \left[\frac{\sum_{i=1}^{m} W_{ij} S_{ij}}{m} \right] \quad (i + 1,2 \ldots.n) \qquad (4)$$

Where $W_{ij}^{1} + W_{ij}^{2} = \cdots = W_{ij}^{3} = 1$

The W_{ij} in equation (4) denotes the weight assigned to *j*th component of SLS index of *i*th region, When weights are identical and sum to unity, then SLS index is estimated as a simple mean. When the weights are different across all *i* and *j*, SLS index is computed as a weighted mean. The former is denoted as Z_{ijk} and the latter as Z_{ik}. Thus all the indices as well as both Z_{ik} and Z_{ijk} vary between 0 to 1.

Three sets of variables, each representing all the three dimensions of SAD are selected. Economic efficiency is represented by the three variables: labour productivity, land productivity and population below poverty line. Ecological security is reflected by three variables: population density, geographical area under forest and per capita availability of ground water. Intergenerational equity is represented by three variables female literacy, per capita consumption of commercial energy, and per capita availability of food grains. Data for three sets of variables pertaining to forty agro-climatic sub-zones are obtained. The sample covered two zones each from Rajstan, Haryana, Karnatak, Kerala, three zones each from Bihar, Andhra, Punjab, UP, Maharastra, Gujrat, Tamil Nadu, West Bengal and four zones each from Orissa and Madhya Pradesh.

The values of Economic efficiency index (E-index), Ecological security index (L-index) and Social equity index (S-index) are estimated and presented in Table 2. It is observed that values of E-index, S-index and L-index vary from 0.895 to 0.115. from 0.845 to 0.258 and from 0.997 to 0.127 respectively. This shows that there is a wide variations in the agricultural system of the sample regions with respect to their economic equity and ecological dimensions. The agriculturally advanced region in Punjab, Haryana and Uttar Pradesh have performed better in terms of economic-efficiency. Karnatak, Kerala, Tamil nadu, Maharastra and Gujrat have performed better in terms of social equity. Mountainous. regions of UP, Kerala, MP and Karnatak have dominated in terms of ecological security index. The SLS index (z) ranges from 0.653 to 0.185 while weighted SLS index (Z*) ranges from 0.611 to 0.136. This indicates that the relatively narrow range of Z and Z* represents the fact that the performance of the region is not consistent across the three aspects of SAD. About one-third of the regions having the SLS index of above 0.5 are located in MP, AP, Punjab, Orissa and Gujrat. Counter intuitively, the regions with better potential for SAD are not in Punjab, Haryana, West Bengal, Kerala, UP but in Orissa, MP, Andhra and Tamil Nadu, as the latter group showed relatively better performance in terms of all the aspects of sustainability.

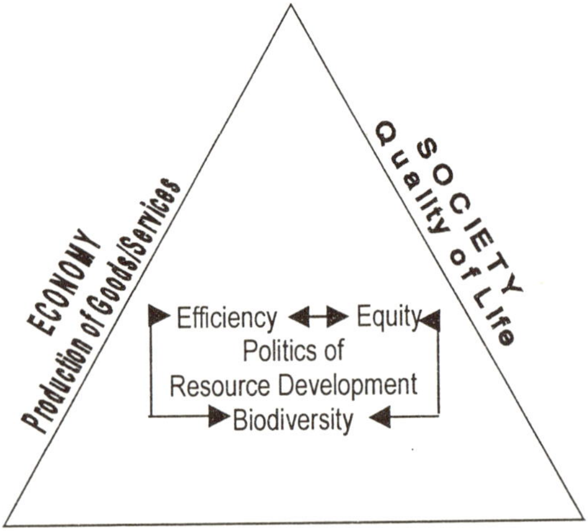

Fig. 2.4: Intergene

The SLS index has policy relevance. It can provide further policy guidance for undertaking specific programmes and projects through which investments can be channeled to improve the overall sustainability of agricultural development. It can help not only to establish inter-regional priority for allocation of agricultural investment but also to priorities programmes and projects of vulnerable regions, which need immediate policy attention.

2.6. LOOKING AHEAD

Table 2.2 : Sustainable Livelehood Security Index

State	*Agroclimatic Zone*	*E-Index*	*Rank*	*S-Index*	*Rank*	*L-Index*	*Rank*	*Sustainable Livelihood Socurity Index (SISI)*			
								Z	*Rank*	*Z**	*Rank*
Orissa	Coastal	0.18	31	0.651	7	0.684	10	0.479	17	0.363	22
	Inland	0.503	13	0.428	26	0.985	2	0.653	1	0.586	2
	Northern Plateau	0.134	39	0.42	27	0.96	3	0.513	13	0.279	29
	South-Western Hills	0.399	15	0.287	38	0.932	5	0.589	4	0.534	3
Bihar	South Bihar Plains	0.158	36	0.382	33	0.282	32	0.229	38	0.218	38
	North-East Plains	0.139	38	0.375	35	0.228	36	0.189	39	0.175	39
	North Bihar Plains	0.166	34	0.302	37	0.127	40	0.185	40	0.135	40
Madhya Pradesh	Chhatisgarh	0.517	12	0.457	23	0.711	7	0.525	10	0.501	5
	Bastar Plateau	0.419	14	0.389	30	0.997	1	0.615	3	0.517	4
	Northern Hills	0.115	40	0.419	28	0.787	6	0.456	21	0.251	34
	Vindya Plateau	0.396	16	0.49	17	0.7	8	0.548	6	0.5	6
Andhra Pradesh	South Coastal	0.674	6	0.589	9	0.665	13	0.621	2	0.611	1
	North Coastal	0.185	29	0.519	16	0.956	4	0.553	5	0.37	20
	Rayalaseema	0.178	32	0.475	20	0.355	21	0.425	26	0.325	25
Punjab	Central	0.895	1	0.686	5	0.235	35	0.518	12	0.422	15
	Northern	0.753	3	0.57	10	0.337	25	0.509	14	0.44	13

State	Agroclimatic Zone	E-Index	Rank	S-Index	Rank	L-Index	Rank	Sustainable Livelihood Socurity Index (SISI)			
								Z	Rank	Z*	Rank
	Southern	0.821	2	0.46	22	0.313	30	0.53	9	0.435	14
Rajsthan	Southern Plains	0.545	9	0.275	39	0.39	18	0.41	28	0.375	19
	Northern arid	0.583	7	0.365	32	0.328	27	0.439	23	0.389	17
Uttar	Eastern Plains	0.213	26	0.387	31	0.178	38	0.279	37	0.221	37
Pradesh	Western Hills	0.219	25	0.487	19	0.678	11	0.48	16	0.421	16
	Central Plains	0.534	11	0.325	36	0.558	16	0.478	18	0.441	12
Mahar-	Central Plateau	0.392	19	0.471	21	0.325	28	0.328	34	0.278	30
astra	Eastern Vidarbha	0.54	10	0.525	14	0.618	14	0.52	11	0.48	7
	Western Hills	0.273	22	0.767	3	0.397	17	0.455	22	0.385	18
Gujrat	South Gujrat	0.31	17	0.651	6	0.695	9	0.543	8	0.478	8
	North Gujrat	0.148	37	0.535	12	0.35	22	0.348	32	0.276	31
	Middle Gujrat	0.19	28	0.596	8	0.341	23	0.383	39	0.316	26
Haryana	Plains	0.688	4	0.378	34	0.24	34	0.438	24	0.36	23
	Arid areas	0.563	8	0.567	11	0.318	29	0.475	10	0.445	11
Karnatak	Central	0.156	35	0.455	24	0.29	31	0.338	33	0.252	33
	Southern	0.678	5	0.489	18	0.378	20	0.503	15	0.475	9
Kerala	Mid lnds	0.287	20	0.845	1	0.245	33	0.477	19	0.375	21

State	Agroclimatic Zone	E-Index	Rank	S-Index	Rank	L-Index	Rank	Sustainable Livelihood Socurity Index (SISI)			
								Z	Rank	Z*	Rank
	Coastal mid lands	0.198	27	0.835	2	0.218	37	0.417	27	0.265	32
Tamil	Northern	0.267	23	0.258	40	0.287	19	0.297	36	0.283	28
Nadu	Central	0.28	21	0.415	29	0.335	26	0.35	31	0.33	24
	Hills Regions	0.3	18	0.76	4	0.56	15	0.545	7	0.473	10
West	Coastal	0.182	30	0.52	15	0.339	24	0.358	30	0.285	27
Bengal	Alluvial	0.263	24	0 53	13	0.149	39	0.312	35	0.242	35
	Tarai	0.175	33	0.445	25	0.67	12	0.426	25	0.23	36

Man is ceaselessly striving for riches. He is enslaved to and obsessed by technological advancement and higher GNP of developmentalism. This obsession has despoiled the environment and is tending to ruin the capacity of the ecosystem to support life. All the while man has been treating the planet as an open system. Natural ecosystem is there to be subdued, to be exploited and even to be enjoyed. The environmental stance is in fact an assault on modernity in all its forms whether capitalist or socialist. There is an apparent incompatibility. Developmentalism and Environmentalism are conflictual. The riddle that mankind faces is how to resolve the Development Environment conundrum. Accepting this challenge involves many shifts and huge costs. But not accepting the challenge spells heavier cost to the posterity. In order to be really able to respond to the challenges of environment-energy crisis, the social order should satisfy three following conditions:

(1) It must conceptualise an integrated global energy system and environmental order.

(2) It must integrate nature into the production mechanism and process of identifying the human needs'.

(3) It must recognise that human being is multi-dimensional and no longer reduce them to uni-dimensional labourers.

RATIONAL CRITERIA

All these three conditions are inextricably linked with each other. The social order in which we live in at both national and global level, is incapable of facing upto these conditions. It is because of the fragmented nature of decision-making and wide disparity among nations. The implementation of environmental protection measures comes into direct conflict with the logic of private accumulation and the underlying international order.

The incorporation of the environmental dimension in the regulation of economic choices is only possible in the context of a decentralised democratic set up with social content. Decentralisation should extend beyond the restricted field of politics into the field of environmental and economic management. It is only under this framework that the individualism can be reconciled with humanism. Now we realise that if man has to exist in this finite system, then he has to operate with the rules of nature, under which he himself has evloved. He has to work within a complex of dynamic inter-related system of which he is an integral part. Therefore, what is urgently required is to develop an intergenerational set of criteria entailed by an ecosystem approach to the resource management. Fig. 4 explains the various intergenerational criteria and components of sustainable growth. Economy, Society and Environment are the three components of sustainable growth. It consists of all the objectives of narrow economic system.

This approach necessarily has to have a decentralised pattern of development. This approach is not anti-life, nor welfare-reducing. Its fundamental objective is total well being of the society at present and in future. This is the only approach, which can ensure a sound and sustainable balance between a productive environment and a protective environment In view of protection and preservation, the negative effect of the rise in material welfare requires reorientation with respect to certain prevailing economic tendencies so that in addition to economic development, the protection of environment and preservation of natural resources have to be conceived of as an explicit aim in planning and in political decision-making. Decentralism is the most appropriate movement which can reconcile the contradiction between developmentalism and environmentalism. Unfortunately there is a current worldwide movement towards free marketism. It is propounded as the correct method to bring balance between developmental objectives and environmental imperatives. It is too optimistic. Market is never friendly to the man nor to the environment. In the market the price is currency notes but in the environment the price is "life". The life lost in the nature cannot be regenerated by cash obtained from the market Market is never friendly to the poor man, vulnerable section nor to the backward regions. Therefore decentralisation is the only process, which can achieve substainable growth. It can ensure spatial, sectoral and operational balance. It creates functional peoples participation and a bottom-up approach to every problem. It emphasises the questions of "empowerment" and "entitlement". It ensures 'entitlement' from below but not endowment from above. It gives 'autonomy' by right but not enthrustment by discretion. It brings a balance among problems, potentials and priorities of local people. is the correct development strategy which can develop the economy consisting of vast unorganised sector and build up the society consisting of vast vulnerable sections. It can instill flexibility to the entire system and facilitate organisational, Institutional reforms according to the environmental imperatives. An integrated planning framework has been illustrated in Fig.5. Environmental objectives are as important as Development objectives in order to determine the policies and strategies for sectoral and spatial planning. Sectoral and spatial planning along with environmental impact Assessment influence the implementation of development activities which should be followed by auditing and evaluation. After auditing and evaluation, through project redesign or process reforms the environmental and developmental objectives are to be redefined. Both the 'need to produce' and 'need to protect' are vitally relevant and indispensable, neither should be compromised. Since no policy can pretend to affect one without influencing the other, both the needs must be taken into account in the policy formulation process and balanced in the ultimate decision-making. Not withstanding the practical difficulties we should be concerned about the problem in its proper dimension and severity. If we really wish to improve the quality of life for us and for the posterity, and not just talk about doing so, we must adopt appropriate public policies in a decentralised framework that may sacrifice at present some efficiency and ordinary growth of GNP to enjoy higher green GNP in terms of inter and intra-generational equity with sustainable development.

REFERENCES

Barbier, E.B. (1989), *Economics, Natural Resources Scarcity and Development,* Earth Scan, London.

Borelli Peter (1988), *Cross Roads: Environmental Priorities for the Future,* Island Press.

Brown, L.R. (1981), *Building a Sustainable Society,* W.W. Norton, New York.

Brown, L.R., et at. (1993), *The State of the World,* Report of the World Watch Institute on Progress towards a Sustainable Society, New York.

Das, Kumar (1988), Ecosystem Approach, *Indian journal of Regional Science,* Vol. XX(1)

—, (1990), *Energy and Rural Economic Development* in *India,* Ashish, Delhi.

—, (1990) Intergenerational Approach for Sustainable Development, Proceedings of 11th International Seminar on Environmental Impact Assessment, held at University of Aberdeen, August

—, (1993), *Environment and Development Conundrum,* Discovery Publishing House, New Delhi (ed.)

—, (1994), Environmental Impact of Industrialisation in Eastern Ghat, Ministry of Environment and Forest, Govt. of India, Delhi.

Goldsmith, E. et al. (1988), *The Earth Report: The guide to global Ecological Issues,* Princeton Sloan.

Hekstra, G.P. (1989), Global Warning and Rising Sea Levels, *The Ecologists,* Vol. 19(1)

Hussain, M. (1994), *Sustainable Development,* RRH Publishing, New Delhi (ed).

Kothan, R. (1982), *Environment and Development in Asia and the Pacific Experiences and Prospects,* UNEP.

Meadows, D.H., et al. (1972), *The Limits to Growth,* Signet, New York.

Murphy, E.P. (1967), *Governing Nature,* Quadrangle Books, Chicago.

Nijkamp, P, et al. (1993), *Dynamic Modeling for Sustainable Development,* Revue European Des Sociales Science, Vol. XXXI (96).

Pearce, P.W. and Atkinson, G. (1992), *Measuring Sustainable Development,* CRERGE University College of London.

Redclift, M. (1987), *Sustainable Development,* Methuen, London

Sam H. Schurr (1972), *Energy, Economic Growth and the Environment,* John Hopkins University Press (ed).

Schneider, S.H. (1989), *Global Warming: Are we entering the Green House Country,* Sierra Club, Boon.

Smith, R.I. (1976), *The Ecology of Man,* Harper and Row, London (ed).

Smith, W.R. (1982), *Energy from Forest Biomass,* Academic Press, New York (ed).

Tobla, M.K. (1984), *Sustainable Development,* Butterworths, London.

Vandana Shiva and J. Bandopadhyay (1988), Political Economy of Ecology Movements, *Economic and Political Weekly,* Vol. XXIII (4), June.

WCED (1987), *Our Common Future,* Oxford Univ. Press, Oxford.

3
Sustainable Growth and Equity

The symptoms of the present economic crisis of India are basically attributable to structural deficiencies and rigidities of the development process that has an inherent tendency to generate macro economic imbalances which have jeopardised the growth process. It is also true that plethora or direct controls over investment, production, prices, imports, foreign capital and even exports have played havoc with the industrial efficiency and therefore, with the process of sustainable development. Rigidity and regulation breeds corruption, which is the biggest, most pervasive and corrosive problem of India. It weakens the links between policy decisions and their implementation. The real problem does not lie anywhere other than "economic rigidity and non-accountability." India has not yet achieved the flexibility in the domestic economic system in order to achieve growth sustainability

The notion of sustainable development can be regarded as a result of the need to solve a potential and/or actual conflict between growth and conservation, with a particular view on efficiency and equity, now and in the future. It recognises the goal of the survival of human species, of the realisation of unacceptable quality of life for each individual in present and future generations, and of a wise management of natural resources and ecosystems, with the help of a broader economic system. Sustainable development highlights the long-term doomsday scenario and puts emphasis on intergenerational equity, economic-ecological integration and regional scale. It shows a compassionate concern for the posterity. It contends that environment and growth are not contradictory. A sound resource base is a prerequisite for sustainable development, which is defined as the progress that seeks to meet the needs and aspirations of the present generation without compromising the ability of future generations to meet their requirements. It reconciles the need for conservation with the need for development at one stroke. It integrates the imperatives of developmentalism and environmentalism. Sustain ability implies at least the maintenance of the level of wellbeing so that it improves the quality of life, but never allows a regression on through time.

But around the globe throughout the history most modern human institutions have evolved in the ways that are at best oblivious and at worst positively hostile to the health of environment. Man's obsession with economic development till today continues to commit two fallacies: (1) It considers the man kind alone and ignores the interdependent system and (2) It treats environment as a commodity.

3.1. FREE MARKETISM

The policy of free marketism has now become a global phenomenon and order of the day. It is the shock therapy of the World Bank. Practically all over the world (except Cuba, North Korea, Myanmar etc.) there is a move towards free market not only in domestic economic activities, but also in foreign economic transactions. This world wide liberalisation and globalisation programme owes its origin to several factors: (1) the external debt crisis in many developing countries, (2) excessive fiscal improvidence and profligacy of developing countries, which resulted in unmanageable foreign exchange deficit, (3) disenchantment with the system of central planning, corruption and inefficiency in developing countries, (4) public disgust with the operations of welfare state in industrialised countries, which led to the rise of Reaganism and Thatcherism, (5) the collapse of socialist regimes in Eastern Europe, and (6) finally, the spectacular growth of income and standard of living of East and South-East Asian countries through market and trade.

It is interesting to note that, at this juncture, there is convergence of views of both North and South. FBM now holds the centre-stage of attention of both groups of economists of advanced, industrial countries and developing countries. The policy of 'free market mechanism' has been proclaimed as the benign means of relieving the West from 'recession' and developing world *from* 'stagnation.' Ardent votaries of this policy advocate as a "Rules of Thumb" for a blind pursuit, which instead of producing desirable effects may result in disastrous consequences for the developing countries (Hossain 1993). Because free marketism may be a necessary condition but not a sufficient condition for the resumption and reignition of economic growth. At best, economic growth may be an assured product of FBM but not sustainable growth. Above all, it is an accepted fact that even sustainable economic growth does not necessarily lead to 'development' in backward economics. Economic indices and social indices are incompatible and inconsistent. Therefore one has to have an uneasy feeling as to the efficacy of this doctrine of shock therapy. It is an experimental path with different institutional framework and operational rules. It is based on myopic and erroneous premises. It is still hooked on to the theory of 'trickle down effect.' High rate of economic growth is believed to automatically solve all other critical issues like unemployment, inequality, poverty and rural development. It is purportedly ordained with the ideology of 'laissez faire,' where even Adam Smith did not contend an undiluted free marketism. Even Smith was advocating for invisible hand (marketisation) subject to the laws of the state and moral codes of the society. Thus, SAP is likely to fail because it is based on naive illusions of high-tech, which is never defined and ignores the fundamental factor of unequal development. There are many complex facets, and hypocrisy and the failure to comprehend it is likely to result in wrong kind of globalisation.

The identical policy reforms accepted as the 'rules of thumb' and applied indiscriminately, is very unwarranted. The policy of devaluation and monetary tightness, for instance, has proved to be appropriate for some Countries and very harmful for some others. The socio-economic impact of SAP is not uniform among social groups, regions and countries. In industrial countries it has raised labour productivity, but in the process it has accentuated the unemployment rate. It has also succeeded in lowering the inflation rate and fiscal deficit. However, so far there is no sign of an improvement in the overall growth rate of output and income in some countries. On the contrary, income disparity among households and regions have tended to rise. In East and South-East Asia it has been successful and has raised the average standard of living of people. On the other hand, the African economics, particularly the Sub-Saharan region, are undergoing the economic retrogression (i.e., rise in poverty, unemployment, malnutrition, disease and infant mortality). In countries of Latin America, there is mixed experience. But in both African and Latin America the liberalisation process has shifted the labour from the organised to the informal sector where the wage rate is very low and social security is absent. Therefore, the impact and efficacy of the current worldwide movement towards market-induced strategies, discarding the old ideologies can not be understood by clubbing all these countries together. One need to distinguish among four groups of countries: (1) Industrially advanced countries, (2) Newly industrialised countries, (3) Erstwhile centrally planned command economies, and (4) Developing economies of the South. The level of development and characteristics of these countries widely differ. With unfettered openness, scrambling to embrace the market is common for all but the driving forces are different for each. The standard FBM-prescriptions are largely meant only for an overheated industrial economy in order to (i) reduce investment demand at home (ii) make exports competitive, and (iii) attract foreign fund to ease BOP Situations. Therefore, SAP has produced desirable results where the preconditions like good infrastructure, low population growth, growth of human capital, high saving and investment rates committed Bureaucracy, improved work culture, general thrust on productivity, efficiency, and discipline are conducive. Where these conditions are not satisfied it results in inequity with or without growth. Even in successful cases, regional disparity has widened, especially in large economies like, China, Brazil and Indonesia.

3.2. REALITIES OF FRIENDLY MARKETS

Let us put an insight into the role and functioning of the global market. In many countries, markets are neither free nor efficient nor equitable. Markets are never friendly to the poor, to the weak and vulnerable, either nationally or internationally. The markets are handmaidens of powerful interest groups and they are greatly affected by the prevailing distribution of income. Markets can not become neutral or competitive in all situations, unless the playing ground is made more even and playable to begin with. Majority is going to fall outside the marketplace because they do not have enough education, health and nutrition to compete on any footing.

Globalisation of markets unfortunately is not friendly to poor nations or poor people. Let us look at some of the dramatic facts that we derive from the Human Development Report about the functioning of global market.

1. The poorest 20% of the world's population receive only 0.2% of the global commercial credit, 1% of the world trade and 2.7% of the global foreign private investment.
2. The real income disparity between the top 20% and bottom 20% of the I world's population has exploded to 150 times by 1990-more than twice the level of 1960 as a result of working of the global market.
3. The indebted countries of Latin America have paid 4 times higher real interest rates in 1980 compared to the industrial countries (17% compared with 4%) because of the major fall in their commodity prices.
4. The share of Sub-Saharan Africa in global trade markets has declined from I 3.8% in 1970 to 1 % in 1989. in spite of many trade concession.
5. The global capital market has worked in such a fashion in the 1980s that the poor nations started transferring $50 billion per annum of net resources to the rich nations every year.
6. The world commodity market has functioned in such a manner that primary commodity prices (except oil) have declined to their lowest levels since great depression. Sub-Saharan Africa alone lost more than $50 billion in export earnings between 1986 and 1990 because of depressed commodity prices.

7. Above all, all developing countries are being denied at least US $500 billion of economic opportunities in the global markets every year because of trade restrictions, immigration controls and uneven capital flows. This is about ten times more than the amount of annual foreign assistance they receive.
8. With the adherence of FB model 24 countries have become losers, out of which 17 are in Sub-Saharan Africa, 5 in Latin America and 2 in Middle East. The growth rate of real *per* capita GDP estimated in 1991 (estimated *for* the economies in the lowest quintile of growth) during 1965-85 are shown in the part thesis corresponding to each country. Afghanistan (-.003), Angola (.028), Argentina (0.001), Benin (-0.004), Central African Rep (-.004), Chad(-.016), Gambia (-.010), Ghana (-.012), Guinea (.000), Guyana (-.005), Kuwait(-.o65),' Liberia (-.008), Madagascar (-.018), Mauritania (-.002), Mozambique (-.029), Nicargua (-.018), Nigeria (-.002), P. New Guinea (.000), Peru (.001), Sengel (-.004), Sirra Leona (- 008), Sudan (.002), Zaire (-.011) and Zambia (-.022).

Thus, we observed that the benefits of the global market have been surreptitiously hijacked by the rich always. It is more comfortable to accept the reality that it is almost impossible to redistribute income and asset more equitably. There are many practical problems, there are several political limits. But we can find no difficulty in distributing knowledge and skill equitably among the countries. It is a tremendous leveling force to enable people to compete in the market. That is why unless there is a tremendous investment in human capital formation in developing countries, the market shall continue to work inefficiently and inequitably.

3.3. REAL ISSUES

Economic reforms are guided by rules of thumb. The under lying general equilibrium model of the economy for which these standard rules, apply is an unrealistic portrayal of most of the developing countries. The model does not seem to address the complex economic structures in developing economies. The model holds good only under very restrictive, assumptions, perhaps only for small economies and not for large ones. It lacks theoretical support and empirical evidence. There are examples of success and failure of both orthodox and heterodox policy initiatives. Developing countries with different historical contexts and institutional set up, varying lines of casualty in their economic systems require different approaches to stabilisation and structural reforms. Be this as it may, factors such as the structural reforms. Be that as it may, factors such as the structure of the existing capital stock, size of population and natural resource endowments put somewhat flexible boundary conditions on policies aimed at raising productive efficiency, but a general solution is non-existent.

With the ongoing process of globalisation and liberalisation the following six pertinent questions may be raised in the context of Indian economy. Can the policy of free marketism

(a) reduce regional inequality?

(b) reduce income inequality?

(c) reduce rural urban disparity?

(d) mitigate gender inequality?

(e) solve unemployment crisis?

(f) ensure inter generational equity?

3.4. REGIONAL INEQUALITY

The protagonists of economic reforms believe that

the agriculture can work as the biggest safety net in the process of adjustment by softening the rigorous of inflation as well as by raising income and employment for the poorer sections of the population. It is misconceived.

It is true that a measure of liberalisation is necessary at this present stage, where further growth of the organised parts of the economy would be left to the markets; but unfortunately a large part of the economy particularly the agricultural sector still remains unorganised and backward. This vast unorganised sector can not be integrated automatically with the mainstream of market-led economy. The problems and constraints associated with the agricultural sector of Indian economy would further worsen with the new economic policy. The root of this incompatibility lies in the growth urban bias and rural neglect (rural-urban dualism).

There is a misconception that the agriculture sector as a whole is a heavily subsidised and pampered sector. When we meaningfully divide the agricultural sector into three sub sectors; (1) Green Revolution (GR) Sector, (2) Non-Green Revolution (NGR) Sector, and (3) Agro Based (AB) Sector, one can easily perceive, the impact of new economic reforms. It is understood that the activities of the AB sector are likely to be of considerable help in increasing exports, creating skill- based opportunities and technological up-gradation in farming. But as regards policies, this sub-sector primarily needs a level playing field like other industries and a legal-cum-regulatory regime, which is completely non-existent.

Green revolution areas have made considerable progress towards modernisation and market linkages. But the major part of the agricultural sector still remained 'non-green.' A sharp contrast has emerged during the planning era, among the GR and NGR areas in terms of rise in production, improvement in the yields and extension of irrigation facilities. The contrast is attributable to a number of factors including soil, climate etc, but the most important factor has been pronounced policy bias towards GR areas (where production has increased by more than 9-fold and its yield has increased by 4-fold). The growth in wheat and rice crop have benefited most from the supportive policies for adoption of new technologies, intensified use of modern technologies inputs and increased availability of dependable irrigation. But as regards the coarse cereals and pulses there is lack of policy support. They are neglected by the policy-makers as well as by the market, as the demand for them is very weak. There are number of institutional barriers inhibiting agricultural growth in NGR areas: Eastern India, dry land areas in central, western and southern parts of India. Fallow and wasteland constitute more than 20% of the total land of these regions.

The NGR sector, so far has received meagre policy support excepting relief and assistance programmes. This subsector usually attracts attention only during the period of distress. Both the endogenous impulses for growth and external forces bringing beneficial changes have been very weak in the areas. With the new economic reforms, the isolation of this sector is likely to be more pronounced and its vulnerability to external events is likely to rise. On the contrary, these areas are likely to be more responsive to all development interventions. These regions need major reforms in infrastructure, markets, credit and cooperatives. Once these preconditions for steady growth are established it would be easier to tackle other problems. They need a wide spectrum of policy regime comprising anti-poverty programmes, provision of infrastructure, improvements in markets and institutions, various schemes of input supply and above all, supportive macro economic policies. The task of developing these areas is to build up a society but not merely investing in the sector of an economy. Thus the withdrawal of the role of government will imply the destruction of the unorganised part of the economy and vulnerable section of the society.

3.5. INCOME INEQUALITY

The New Economic Policy, which has been designed in the tune of SAP, overlooks various social objectives such as eradication of poverty, greater emphasis on public sector, faster expansion of basic and key goods, prevention of concentration of economic power in private hands, regional balance and promotion of small industries and *khadi* and village Industries etc. It rather runs counter to all these objectives.

At this stage of industrial development in India at least one can not afford to:

(i) forget that there are many supply side bottlenecks; and

(ii) regard distribution merely as an offshoot of the development process.

All strategies for economic development and policies for combating backwardness, poverty, unemployment, inequality, stagnation etc. are constantly being distorted by the new political and bureaucratic practice. It is a kind of trial and error method having no theoretical foundation nor empirical evidence. It is very difficulty to achieve rapid industrial development with existing supply side constraints, which have to be removed by lone; term deliberate planning. The existing resources can not be readily converted into foreign exchange simply by fiscal restraints and sound exchange rate policy. One can not throw the body with the bath water with the excitement about the new economic thinking. On the contrary a society as prismatic and unequal as India's simply cannot afford to regard distribution merely as an offshoot of development process. The development process has to have a very clear accent on raising the productivity of all classes and particularly of the weaker and poorer sections of the society.

Simultaneous attempts towards stabilisation and economic liberalisation may lead neither to macro economic stability nor to the restoration of growth sustainability. 'Trickle down effect' of SAP shall be more than neutralised by corruption, bureaucratisation, unemployment, industrial unrest and low productivity. These problems can not be handled by 'safety nets,' Draconic and abrupt removal of protection is likely to spell disaster for many large scale and small-scale industries. The industrial sector of the economy is likely to drift into stagnation with low industrial growth and high inflation, which will further aggravate the poverty profile of the economy. Unsuccessful fiscal compression is likely to create 'doublesqueeze' and fail to yield the expected reduction in government's fiscal deficit. It will produce; (i) joblessness in the industrial sector; and (ii) price rise of essential goods. Therefore, SAP is likely to lead to continued stagnation rather than a meaningful structural adjustment. It will fail to bring the majority of rural poor into the vortex of economic development.

3.6. UNEMPLOYMENT PROBLEM

As an answer to the third question raised above it can be said here that the large scale centralised approach with its heavy emphasis on capital-intensive industrialisation shall take most of the investible capital. This approach has never raised the volume employment and has never served the poor. The type of industrialisation that the (NEP) contemplates is not going to be of any benefit to the rural poor. Industrial growth and employment are not related to each other. During 1983-88, Planning Commission of India itself admitted that highest growth rate is associated with lowest growth of employment. The SAP and NEP are not stunned to increasing employment in the small-scale sector. At the most, it may generate very few job opportunities, for highly skilled people. Industries shall require labour which can not be supplied by the village poor. It produces the goods which they do not consume. Hence the industrial activity is mostly labour- displacing. All types of ancilliary industries are likely to be preempted and a type of vicious process of reindustrialisation is likely to set in.

The FBM seeks ostensibly for creating more space for private enterprises. But attractive market incentives for capital formation is only a necessary but not sufficient condition for resumption of private investment and industrial development. All efforts are misguided to promote the growth of 'finance capital' and 'portfolio investment' at the cost of industrial capital and at the cost of investment in agriculture and infrastructure. Promotion of 'finance capital' is likely to shore up speculative activities rather than sustained industrialisation. Therefore, SAP is unlikely to bring neither 'allocative efficiency' nor 'productive efficiency.' There is no theoretical support or empirical evidence as to the effect of liberalisation on economic growth. At the most, Indian market may remain as a captive market for the recession-ridden countries. Market forces may fail to unleash forces for growth and at the most it tends to generate low-income activities horizontally.

The unbridled entry of MNCs now enjoy complete administrative, bureaucratic and political patronage in India. It is a deadly alliance which tends to drag India into a neo-colonial dependency. Acceptance of globalisation slogan is pushing the economy headlong into a set or policies which is in a way irreversible. By giving primacy to the role of MNCs in the bid to attract foreign investment all considerations of investment for the economy in terms of satisfaction of mass needs and self-reliant growth have been extinguished. This fits perfectly well with art investment pattern and production structure to sub serve a social milieu and life style which has no relevance for the broad mass of the people and at the same time impedes the progress towards economic self-reliance. Globalisation without adequate preparedness would be tantamount to opening up the Indian Economy to unfair competition. The adjustment programme is likely to be countered productive. There is no dearth or example of countries, following' the path of structural readjustment, have all suffered substantial deterioration in the terms of trade. The outcome of SAP has ranged from moderately successful to disastrous. One should not feel excited with the examples of Eastern Tigers. The success of South Korea, Taiwan, Singapore, it should be remembered, to a large extent is attributable to the role of the state, which developed the necessary infrastructure, human resources, and intervened in the process of resource allocation so as to achieve overall development. Newly industrial countries are the most indebted countries of the Third world (Amin, 1995). They are the real peripheries of enclave market of the developed world. On the other hand one should observe the deadly consequence of FBM with Argentina, Bolivia, Peru, Morocco, Syria, Venezuela, Brazil, Mexico and many other African and Latin American Countries.

Growth of GDP in 1992 of Brazil, Peru, Ivory Coast and Mexico are -0.9, -2.8, -0.3, 2.6 respectively. Inflation rates in 1992 over the previous year in Brazil, Peru, Turkey, are 1008%, 74%, 70% and 69% respectively. Real wage has fallen (1984=100) to 76.2, 72.6, 70.5, 87.9 respectively in Argentina, Brazil, Peru, Tanzania. Thus, the adjustment with human face is another fanciful rhetoric to cajole people at large.

3.7. GENDER INEQUALITY

The division of labour by gender within the household of developing countries is stubbornly cultural. Women as a class are oppressed and subdued by the hegemony of social patriarchy. The gender inequality is very sharp with the rural households. Since the employment options available to the rural women are severely limited and since the opportunities for skill acquisition and job mobility are more limited for the rural female than the male, the work for women has come to mean back-breaking toil, endless drudgery and humiliation. High work force participation for the poor female in the rural areas means the relentless weariness of too heavy workloads and the deprivation of childhood care and schooling for their children (particularly for the girl-child) The dividing line between productive work and domestic work is not only arbitrary but also tends to under estimate the women's contribution to domestic work. The rural woman as a class is saddled with 'triple burden.' If one takes into account the unpaid word, in these countries, women in poor households work much longer hours and have no or less leisure time than their male counterparts. The votaries of SAP argue that now there is a trend of continued feminisation of employment in all developing countries. It does not reflect the sign of progress or prosperity. It does not imply the success of FBM or emergence of new technological break-through or improvement in the efficiency of the secondary sector either. But there are two major reasons which have led to the feminisation of work: (i) the structural shift of employment from manufacturing to service sector activities in these countries, and (ii) the incidence of poverty (economic strain on households inflicted by the double squeeze) and the question of survival.

The present economic reforms, particularly in the Third world countries are likely to promote (1) highly sophisticated technology and (2) create imperfections in the rural factor (particularly labour) market. These two factors tend to continuously displace the female workers from high productive activities to low productive activities. It is tending to accentuate the concentration of women in domestic works and non-market roles and activities. The globalisation of prices (not income) is likely to spell further economic strain on women, in term of work burden and curtailment of family expenditures. Therefore, feminisation of work is likely to result in feminisation of poverty and promote the process of housewifisation further.

3.8. INTERGENERATIONAL EQUITY

Intergenerational equity is implied by the global concern for environmental crisis. The success of free marketisation policy is wholly misconceived from the environmental point of view. It is in fact tending to generate industrialisation process which is not environmental-friendly. No matter, what type of SAP is adopted, the process of extraction, mining and rapid large scale industrialisation is certainly going to pose problems of environmental degradation. Historically economic expansion has led to the reckless exploitation of natural resources with little or no concern for their renewal. Therefore, one point is very clear, that is, 'developmentalism' and 'environmentalism' are incompatible and conflictual to each other. It is an obvious thing that the system which is market-friendly can never be environment friendly. Therefore, in the context of 'free marketism' the concept of environment-friendly development is a myth.

Unfortunately, the concern for environment has emerged from the Western world (after their free riding), from where the incessant urge for developmentalism has manifested. The advocates of developmentalism are very optimistic. They hold that exhaustion of natural resources and environmental crisis simply an event but not at all a disaster. Protagonists of SAP propose market as solutions to ecological crisis. Globalisation shall enhance the exploitation of natural resources with high capital investment, which helps in conservation of resources. They argue that modern scientific development shall take care of depletion and degradation of natural resources. On the contrary the votaries of environmentalism contend that as population tends to surge ahead, the world is heading towards a catastrophe. The natural resources and the environment which is already burdened by the present population growth will simply collapse under the weight of the demand and pressure of future population growth. But in reality the environmental crisis is neither as grim as the pessimists believe nor as rosy as the optimists claim. The most plausible outcome is that we are feeding ourselves at the cost of our children and grand children. The over-ploughing, over pumping intensified use of al! natural resources, in an attempt to survive is possible, only in the short run. But in the long run the dietary intake will creep in, food availability shall fluctuate, crop shall become more vulnerable to pests, weather will fluctuate. And the fact remains that the atmospheric concentration of carbon dioxide has increased by 25% over the past century and oxygen is not growing at double that rate. The ozone is becoming depleted. There is rapid increase in green house effect and global warming. Flotillas of garbage ride the currents of every ocean. Acid rain is killing lakes of every continent. Dozen of species become extinct every month as a result of the expansion of deserts in one hemisphere and denudation of forests in another hemisphere.

It is true that many types of equipment and preventive measures are available which can mitigate the adverse effects of the industrial process on environment.

But these processes and equipment are very expensive and frequently not even available to developing countries. This problem has further worsened because knowledge is being treated as a private property in the new patent regime. Modernisation and upgradation of traditional methods of production are often environment-friendly. But it can be achieved only under a regulated regime. Modern science makes it possible through decentralised production processes which are necessarily environment-friendly. But it itself is a function of knowledge. Without globalisation of knowledge and scientific development, the ongoing SAP can only lead to further intensification of the harnessment of natural resources and deterioration of the environmental standards. With the extension of the domain of patentability the contemplated SAP shall lead to globalisation of ignorance but not globalisation of scientific discoveries. Free dissemination of knowledge which today reposes with the developed countries is an essential prerequisite for ensuring environment-friendly development. The ground reality is that the developing countries are now at the stage of underdevelopment. Their intervention and harnessment of environmental resources is likely to be more in the future. As their income level has remained very low, they can not afford to pay attention to the quality of life, the condition of the habitat and imbalance in the ecosystem of themselves nor for their posterity. When the billions of poor people in developing countries can not be denied of their basic requirement for their survival in an era of mass consumption, the consequences of this seems to be very dismal for the whole world in the shape of environmental degradation. The pattern of production and consumption which would be environment-friendly necessarily calls for regulation, government intervention and planning. It can never emerge from the interplay of market forces. The free play of market forces especially in an economic system with a highly iniquitous distribution of income and wealth can not bring about an environment-friendly pattern of development.

The contemplated Economic Growth, in the SAP tends to cause over exploitation of natural resources. Because it is a fact that all capital intensive technologies are energy intensive, if not pollution intensive. The multinational businessmen tend to be oblivious of the consequences to the society, in their scrambling for profit maximisation. Therefore, it is a obvious thing that they never adopt environmentally sound business practices, which reduce emissions, prevent' wastes, consume energy and natural resources. Scarcity of natural resources shall ultimately lead to crisis of survival for all living being. Growth of market can not solve the very crisis it creates. Natural resources can be converted into cash but cash can never be converted into nature's ecological processes. Those who offer market solutions, to environmental crisis limit their thinking. horizon to the market only. They look forward for inventions of substitutes and to the commercial function of natural resources as commodities and raw materials. However, in natures' economy, the currency is not money but life (both of human and other living species). The increased availability of financial resources cannot regenerate the life lost in the nature through ecological destruction. It is a fact that the economic growth based on unsustainable resource-use can not continue indefinitely. It has a built-in-doom. It endangers the carrying capacity of the planet and despoils the life support system. Therefore, the government has a positive role to curb all pollution- intensive activities and energy-intensive activities. It has to encourage energy efficiency and waste minimisation and develop flexible, cost-effective regulatory programmes. Healthy economy and healthy environment do not go together. Thus, if we want to have an environment-friendly pattern of development but not just talk about doing so, state intervention is inescapable. The extent that SAP is attuned to globalisation of the economy and reliance on marketisation one can neither think of simple development in general nor environment-friendly development in particular.

Thus, the answers to above six issues are consistently negative. The transition for the economy as backward as Indian Economy, which suffers from: rigidities in various fronts, macro economic instability and imbalances, non-accountability, bureaucratism and corruption at all levels is likely to only foster the interest of modern capitalism. Therefore, the future implications of economic reforms are dismal in terms of the real issues of equity in developing countries. We are putting the cart before the horse. Development after a point generates and reinforces the need for globalisation but not vice versa. Globalisation without development is likely to lead to the ossification of the structure of underdevelopment. The policy of globalisation for India is premature and misconceived rather than wrong. There are many inherent contradictions, illusions, irrelevance and hypocrisy in the new economic model. It is based on wrong and myopic premises. It does not address the real questions that affect the Indian economy. It puts over emphasis on efficiency and modern industrial sector at the cost of rural sector (Where majority ekes out their living) and equity aspects.

One must always remember one simple thing that the salvation of the developing economy as vast and diverse as India's, lies only in the transformation and revitalisation of its rural economy, which requires extensive role of the public sector and which makes the role of the state inescapable. One's sense of idealism is in direct proportion to one's distance from the real scenario. Even the best judgment of the rich and the best model of the Harvard,

Oxford, Yale and Washington can not always reflect and accommodate the harsh realities, potentials and priorities of the majority of the population of the developing world.

3.9. LOOKING AHEAD

The symptoms of the present economic crisis of India are basically attributable to structural deficiencies and rigidities of the development process that has an inherent tendency to generate macro economic imbalances which have jeopardised the growth process. It is also true that plethora or direct controls over investment production, prices, imports, foreign capital and even exports have played havoc with the industrial efficiency and therefore, with the process of economic development. Rigidity and regulation breeds corruption, which is the biggest, most pervasive and corrosive problem of India. It weakens the links between policy decisions and their implementation. The real problem does not lie anywhere other then "economic rigidity and non-accountability." India has not yet achieved that flexibility in the domestic economic system in order to reap the benefits of the internationalisation process.

Thus, many developing countries of the world including India, instead of mindlessly marching with the new economic reforms, requires a type of structural reforms, before opening up its economy to the competitive regime, which should have ensured:

(i) Higher standard of living to the village people,

(ii) Production for mass-consumption,

(iii) Organisational and institutional reforms,

(iv) Bureaucratic and political reforms,

(v) Educational reforms and effective programme for skilling, and

(vi) Use of labour-intensive technology.

On proper diagnosis, Indian economy is carelessly marching on a 'knife-edge balance' with great risk and uncertainty. Hence, at this juncture India instead of following the new path must adopt a policy of decentralism in order to ensure intra-generational equity and Ecosystem approach in order to achieve sustainable growth and intergenerational equity.

REFERENCES

1. Barbier E.B., 0989), *Economics, Natural Resources Scarcity and Development* Earth Scan, London.
2. Borelli Peter, 0983), *Cross Roads: Environmental Priorities for the Future,* Island Press.
3. Brown L.R., 0981), *Building a Sustainable Society,* WW Norton, New York.
4. Brown L.R., et al., (1993), *The State of the World,* Report of the World Watch Institute on Progress towards a Sustainable Society.
5. Das Kumar 0988) Ecosystem Approach, *Indian Journal of Regional Science* Vol. xx 0).
6. ———*(1990) Energy and Economic Development in India,* Ashish Pub, Delhi.
7. ———*(1990)* Intergenerational Approach for Sustainable Development, *Proccedings of 11th International Seminar on Environmental Impact Assessment, held at University of Aberdeen,* August.
8. ———(1993) *Environment and Development Conundrum,* Discovery Publishing House, New Delhi.
9. ———. (1994) *Environmental Impact of Industrialisation Eastern Ghat,* Ministry of Environment and Forest, Govt. of India, New Delhi.
10. Goldsmith E., et al. (1988) *The Earth Report: the Guide to Global Ecological Issues,* Princeton, Sloan.
11. Hekstra G.P., (1989) *Global Warming and Rising Sea Levels,* The Ecologist Vol. (19(1).
12. Hussain M., (1994) *Sustainable Development,* RPH Publishing, New Delhi (ed).
13. Kothari R., (1982) *Environment and Development in Asia and the Pacific: Experiences and Prospects,* UNEP.

14. Meadows D.H., et al.(1972) *The Limits to Growth*, Signet, New York.
15. Murphy E.P., 0967) *Governing Nature*, Quadrangle Books, Chicago.
16. Nijkamp P., et al. (1993) Dynamic Modeling for Sustainable Development, *Revue European Des Sociales Science*, Vol. XXXI, (96). '
17. Pearce P.W., and Atkinson G (1992) *Measuring Sustainable Development*, CRERGE, University College of London.
18. Redclift M (1987) *Sustainable Development*, Methuen, London.
19. Sam H Schurr (1972) *Energy, Economic Growth and the Environment*, John Hopkins University, Press, (ed).
20. Schneider SH (1989) *Global Warming: Are We Entering the Green House Country*, Sierra Club, Boon.
21. Smith RL (1976) *The Ecology of Man, Harper and Row*, London (ed).
22. Smith WR (1982) *Energy from Forest Biomass*, Academic Press, New York (ed).
23. Tobia MK (1984) *Sustainable Development*, Butterworths, London.
24. Vandana Shiva and J. Bandopadhay (1988) *Political Economic of Ecological Movements*. *Economic and Political Weekly*, Vol. xxiii (24) June.
25. WGED (1987) *Our Common Future*, Oxford Univ. Press, Oxford.

4

Environmental Externality and Common Property Resources

The economic aspects of environmental quality have increasingly drawn the attention of economists particularly from the side regional economics and welfare economics. As a result of their joint efforts gradually a new branch of Environmental Economics has emerged. This new discipline emphasises on the exhaustion of natural resources, economics of pollution, and environmental quality. This branch is defined as a scientific study of scarcity aspects of behaviour of man in relation to his natural, physical and residential surroundings. Environmental economics is involved in the study of both intended and unintended consequences of all production, consumption and all kinds of human intervention into the environment. It studies the trade off problem between environmental quality and economic quantity. It attempts to achieve the tradeoff between environmental goods and other scarce goods. It has distinct economic dimensions, since the cost of obtaining more environmental quality has to be evaluated against the sacrifice of other economic goods. So it aims at integrating the classical goals of dealing with scarcity into the modern problems of environmental quality. It gives new impulses both to economic decision making and to the solution of the environmental dilemma by seeking for a continuous balance between economic development and environmental sustainability. Therefore a prerequisite for a meaningful analysis is the availability of information on ecosystem and economic impacts.

4.1. MATERIAL BALANCE MODEL

The obsession of economic development has not only rewarded the mankind with large scale and variety of products but also brought mass of byproducts such as wastes and pollution. By explaining the well-known material balance model one can obtain more insight into the relationships between economic activities and ecological effects. The material balance model is a formal representation of the s between economic, technical and ecological processes. It arises from the first law of thermodynamics of physics concerning the conservation of matter. It states that in spite of numerous transformation processes in the course of production or consumption no matter is destroyed. Apart from generation of energy there is physical balance between inputs and outputs in all transformation processes. In the following chart it is seen that all production activity obtains all material inputs from the environment and transforms them for final consumption and residuals. The consumption sector itself creates wastes as well as residual s for recycling. It depicts that the environment acts as a source for material inputs and as a destination for waste products. The law of conservation of matter and energy states that the physical masses of all inputs are identical in amount to the residual wastes.

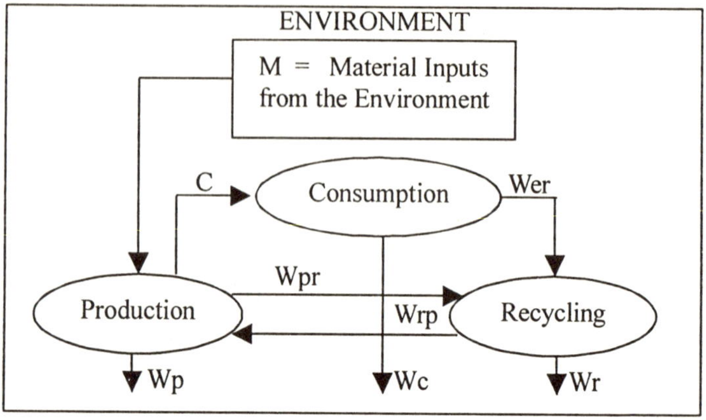

Fig. 4.1: Material Balance Model

We get two identities from the above flow chart;

$$M = Wp + C$$

$$C = Wc + Wr$$

Thus $$M = Wp + Wc + Wr$$

$$= \Sigma Wi, \text{ where: } i = 1,2,3$$

It shows that all-human activity results in wastes, which cause environmental loading. So the notion of final consumption is misleading. Global scale of this notion makes Boulding's concept of 'spaceship earth' very clear. The environment has very large but finite capacity to provide natural resources for all human activities and to absorb waste residuals. When these residuals exceed the waste assimilative capacity and extractions exceed the nature's regenerative capacity then we cause actual and potential damage to the environmental health.

4.2. ENVIRONMENTAL POLLUTION

Environmental pollution refers to the unfavourable alternation of our natural surroundings, partly or wholly as a by-product of man's action. A pollutant is defined as anything, living or non-living or any physical agent that in its excess makes any part of the environment undesirable. In other words a pollutant has been defined as any solid, liquid or gaseous substance present in such concentration as may be or tend to be injurious to the living beings and to the general environment. Pollution necessarily implies a damage to the environment. Such damage is generally described in biological and ecological terms but not necessarily quantifiable in economic terms. There are two types of pollution:

(a) Non Degradable (toxic material like, mercury, DDT etc). They exert negative influence on the ecosystem. Their presence is environmentally detrimental. So all non-degradable materials are pollutants. It can be denoted symbolically as input output function. Let the function be

$$E = f(P) \qquad \ldots 1$$

Where E is the output vector of energy available and P is the input vector of toxic pollutants. In case of non-degradable pollutants we have:

$$\partial E_I / \partial P_J < 0 \qquad \ldots 2$$

where: $i = 1, 2 \ldots\ldots\ldots n$ and $j = 1, 2 \ldots\ldots\ldots m$

(b) Degradable (materials like domestic sewage). They can be decomposed by biological or mechanical treatment. They become pollutants only if

$$\partial E_i / \partial P_j \leq 0 \qquad \ldots 3$$

Environment will not be adversely affected only if

$$\partial E_i / \partial P_j > 0 \qquad \ldots 4$$

If it is positive then the environment will suffer no damage or the stability of the ecosystem will not be affected.

Pollution is considered to be relevant only when it has implications for human welfare. Any kind of environmental damage is linked up with human welfare because a clean environment is vitally significant for both present and future living. So, as soon as the critical conditions (2 and 3) are met, economic evaluation of effects of both biodegradable and non-degradable materials is warranted. Only when the critical limits are surpassed, then the problems of assessment of environmental degradation and externalities emerge.

4.3. TRAGEDY OF COMMONS:

Some of the natural resources are termed as "common property Resources". They are jointly available in the same quantity. But some goods or resources may possess the property of non-excludability even when the benefits occurring from them are subtractive. Public goods possess the characteristics of non-excludability and indivisibility. Non excludability implies fee access to all and indivisibility implies that benefits are not subtractive but of the nature of collective consumption. Examples of CPR are ground water, crude oil reserves, grazing land, and village forests, fishing in village pond and river or marine fishing. CPR is the resource accessible to the whole community, to which no individual has exclusive property right. This definition is useful in focusing on the essential difference between private property based resources and those to which community access is available. It hinges on the fact that private property is on the right to exclude persons other than the owner from the use of such resources, a characteristic that common property do not possess. Runge (1986) has emphasised that common property as an institution must be distinguished from fee and open access where there are no rules regulating individual rights. The absence of any rules for the management of resources would result in fugitive resources and open access resources. Thus a resource becomes common property only when a group of people who have the right to its collective use is well defined and when the rules that govern their use are set out clearly and followed universally. Hence common property resources can be defined as resources which could be simply described as community's natural resources where every member has access and usage facility with specified obligation, without any body having exclusive property right over them. To reiterate, for day to day survival, socio-economic, cultural and occupational need etc, people depend on the land, water, space resources etc, available in the village surrounding other than the land or properties they own until they have access to them. The properties and resources usually existent with in the jurisdiction of the villages of India. Ownership right to all the categories of land and properties belong to the revenue department. But villager uses them until they are allowed. But the degree of dependency on these resources is very high among the backward communities of the backward regions.

Here we attempt to specify the production function for such resources, derive the natural growth curve of a renewable natural resource and highlight the issue of environmental sustainability. Renewable natural resource faces dual problem of conservation and development. Conservation may be defined as an approach to resource management that seeks to leave the resources relatively untouched. Development on the other hand amounts to the use and modification of natural resources. It may involve transformation of the resources. It is considered as a renewable resources because with proper management it can be made to yield direct services indefinitely into the future. But its renewability does not imply that it is free from pressing problem of total depletion and over exploitation.

$$F = \text{Fish Population}$$

We can examine the problem of depletion of natural resources with respect to the fuel wood sector or fishery sector. The characteristics of these resources that make it different from other resources are those that relate to the problems of renewability, ownership and externalities. Despite these differences fish is subject to the operation of price mechanism in the same way as all other resources. So the question that arises here: Can the price system lead to a level of exploitation that will allow the maintenance of a desirable level of stock for the future? All renewable resources including fish are those resources that are subject to a natural rate of growth and therefore are capable of yielding a sustained level of production into the future. The important characteristics of fish is that the rate of its renewal directly depend on the amount of the resource left unharvested. The rate of rise of its population consists of its rate of growth less its mortality rate. The rate of growth of its population can be considered to be directly proportional to the stock of fish. It gives a linear function. In the absence of any harvest population will expand exponentially. But expansion is arrested by mortality factors such as food shortage, predation and diseases. It can be assumed that there is a maximum population which the environment can support equal to Pm. With lower quantity of Population natural mortality rate is also low. As population increases mortality rate increases at an increasing rate. As the maximum population quantity is approached food shortages and diseases etc become more important factors which cause high mortality rates. Mortality is represented by curvi-linear curve. Therefore the natural rate of growth of the species is obtained by subtracting both the curves. After doing this we get the natural growth curve of NGC which is concave downwards. It shows that a sustainable yield can be achieved for any level of resource quantity, provided the rate of harvest does not exceed the rate of change in its population. Sustainable yield therefore refers to the maximum amount that can be harvested from a given stock without decreasing its level in the next period or for future.

Population increases above zero rate of growth. Its growth reaches maximum level at og* and fish increases to P_n. Beyond that level the rate of growth falls with further rise in the population. At lower level of population there is plenty of food and space for their growth. So there is rapid rise in their stock. With higher growth of population the scarcity of food and space force down the rate of growth eventually to zero level at P_m. So ecological restraints automatically impose zero population growth on the species. If the species fail to reproduce themselves above the zero level then the natural growth curve will be the dotted curve. Here there is a critical minimum level of the population below which it disappears. Here the critical minimum level of the species is OP_c below this level it can not maintain a viable rate of renewal. If man does not exploit any thing of the resource the natural equilibrium will be Pm which is a stable equilibrium point.

If $\quad P > P_m$

Then ecological restraints will force the species back to Pm level

If $\quad P < P_m$

Then the ecological factors will be conducive to sustain increase upto P_m.

The natural growth curve implies that with proper management policies it should be possible to harvest the resources annually in such a way that is subject to natural fluctuations, a constant level of population is maintained. The economic importance of the **ngc** lies in the fact that it can be used for determining the exact level of harvesting that will allow a sustainable yield and a constant level of the population. It is perceived easily by understanding the relationship between growth rate and amount of harvesting of the resource:

The Production function of the CPR is denoted as:

$$V_t = f(P_t, E_t)$$

Where: V_t is the harvest level in t time

F_t is the CPR stock in t time

E_t is the Harvesting effort in t time and

$$0 < V < V\max$$

4.4. ENVIRONMENTAL EXTERNALITY

Externality is a meaningful expedient to come to grips with environmental issues. Environmental externalities are non -market effects (positive or negative) which result as a side effect of economic activities of producers, consumers and other economic agents (including the governmental activities) and which affect the welfare or profit conditions of other households through spillovers via man's surroundings. All these externalities have two important characteristics: Interdependency and non-compensation. The first refers to the interaction and connectedness of the decisions and objective functions of various agents. The second refers to refers to a situation where one who creates the damage is not obliged to pay for it, nor who creates some environmental benefit is completely rewarded for it. Another important property of environmental externality emphasised by Mishan (1971), who states that the environmental spillover is frequently unintended or an incidental by product of some otherwise legitimate activity It is a very useful concept in studying the environmental problems, as far as it is related to the non -market actions or unpriced effects. It is the cause of divergence between private profit and social benefit. Consequently it is the cause of failure perfect competition to ensure the optimality. This provides the theoretical insight into the causes and welfare implications of environmental decay and into the way in which environmental policies are placed in the framework of conventional economic thinking. A basic problem is the frequent lack of operationality of the externality approach.

Externalities are classified according to (non-) reparability, (non-) reciprocity, (infra-) marginality and potential (ir-) relevance. Externalities between economic subjects are separable, if their marginal preference with respect to their decision variables are independent of the level of the decision variables of the others actors. Separable externalities can be explained by assuming two entrepreneurs having their interdependent cost functions as follows:

$$C_a = f_1 (Q_a, Q_b) \qquad \text{... 5a}$$

$$C_b = f_2 (Q_b, Q_a) \qquad \text{... 5b}$$

Where Qa, and Q_b represent the production volumes of both the producers. When both are maximising their profit, the first order necessary condition, according to neo classical economic principles, is price equals marginal cost ie.

$$P_a = \partial C_a / \partial Q_a$$

and $$P_b = \partial C_b / \partial Q_b \qquad \text{... 6}$$

Where $\partial C_j / \partial Q_i$ is the marginal cost of ith firm with respect to Q_i. When the social benefit (ie aggregate profit) is to be optimised, decision rule becomes significantly different

$$Pa = \frac{\partial C_a}{\partial Q_a} + \frac{\partial C_b}{\partial Q_b} \qquad \text{... 7a}$$

and $$P_b = \frac{\partial C_b}{\partial Q_b} + \frac{\partial C_a}{\partial Q_b} \qquad \text{... 7b}$$

Where $\partial C_j / \partial Q_i$ represents the marginal cost of *j*th firm with respect to the output decision of *i*th firm. As a result the profit maximisation by individual firms does not lead to the maximum social profit (benefit). Presence of externalities prevents the market to be efficient. In this situation, marginal cost of the producer does not correctly measure the opportunity cost of producing it, so that there is a divergence between marginal social cost and marginal private cost.

In case of non-separable externalities the firms marginal cost are affected by production decisions and resulting environmental damages of the firms. Suitable example of such case is the pollution of the river, the water of which is used by the water supply-company. Here the marginal cost of Water Supply Company is a direct function of the degree of water pollution and thus the level of output of the polluting firm. Therefore it affects the firms optimal decision concerning production level and product mix. Thus the private output decision of *i*th firm is codetermined by the output level of *j*th firm. Thus the existence of non-separable externality does not result in a parallel shift of the firm's cost curve like that of separable externality. Here changes in the value of externality causes the cost curve to shift with different slopes. This implies that the neoclassical rule of price equals marginal cost is difficult to adopt for the individual producer. Moreover it is very complicated to derive the optimal solution for ensuring a optimum social benefit, since Qi can not be solved unambiguously from equation 7. On the contrary if we assume two producers having interdependent market behaviour (Cournot hypothesis) an equilibrium solution for maximum social benefit can be derived by solving Q_a and Q_b simultaneously from equation -7. In a similar way the leader-follower situation from the theory of duopolistic market behaviour (Stackelberg hypothesis) can be applied in order to obtain the equilibrium condition.

We here attempt to make an illustrative exposition of environmental externalities. Let us assume that there are two firms employing labour and capital as their factor inputs. Given the Product and factors Prices, both firms adopt marginal principle for optimal resource allocation. The production function of both producers are

$$V_1 = f_1(X_1, Y_1) \quad \text{... 8a}$$

$$V_2 = f_2(X_2, Y_2) \quad \text{... 8b}$$

So, $$V_i = f_i(X_i. Y_I) \quad \text{... 8c}$$

Where, V_1 and V_2 are production volumes of Firm A and B respectively, X and Y are labour and capital inputs used by both the firms. When degree of homogeneity of both these production functions is one, Euler's theorem is valid in the absence of externalities. The total scale elasticity is unity. i.e

$$\frac{\partial V_i X_i}{\partial X_i V_i} + \frac{\partial V_i Y_i}{\partial Y_i V_i} = 1 \quad \text{... 9}$$

Where: $i = 1, 2$

$$e_{xI} + e_{yI} = 1 \quad \text{... 10}$$

Total wage W_i to be paid by any firm is:

$$Wi = wi .Xi$$

$$= Pi .(\partial Vi / \partial Xi) .Xi \quad \text{... 11}$$

Where: w_i = wage rate and P_i = product price of *i*th firm

By substituting the partial elasticity of output with respect to labour (9) in (11), one gets

$$W_i = P_i V_i e_{xi} = R_i . e_{xi} \quad \text{... 12}$$

where R= total revenue

Total payments for capital is

$$K_i = R_i e_{yi} \quad \text{... 13}$$

So that the total factor payment becomes

$$K_i + W_i = R_i (e_{xi} + e_{yi}) = R_i \quad \text{... 14}$$

Let us assume that one firm inflicts environmental

damage to the other firm, so that the production volume of firm A diminishes, depending upon the level of production of firm B and its environmental externalities. In this case of unidirectional non-separable externalities the production function of the firm A becomes:

$$V_1 = f^1(X_1, Y_1, V_2) \qquad \ldots 15$$

Where as the production function of firm B remains unaffected

$$V_2 = f^2(X_2, Y_2) \qquad \ldots 16$$

By improving the technological efficiency firm A can neutralise the negative effects of this externality. If we still assume 1st degree homogeneity of the production function, then scale elasticity is still unity i.e.

$$\{e_{x1} + e_{y1} + e_{21}\} = 1 \qquad \ldots 17$$

$$\text{where, } e_{21} = \frac{\partial V_1, V_2}{\partial V_2, V_1}$$

It shows the damage inflicted by B firm on A firm. Obviously it is negative as every rise in the volume of production of firm B adversely affects the firm A. Now the problem is how this environmental externality affect the allocation rules for factor payments.

The factor payment of firm A are respectively equal to the marginal net social products according to (12) and (13)

$$K_1 = e_{y1} R_1 \qquad \ldots 18$$

$$\text{and} \quad W_1 = e_{x1} R_1 \qquad \ldots 19$$

Thus total factor payments are:

$$K_1 + W_1 = (e_{x1} + e_{y1}) R_1 = (1 - e_{21}) R_1 \qquad \ldots 20$$

So there is a surplus in factor payment due to the existence of negative environmental externality

$$L = - e_{21} R_1 \qquad \ldots 21$$

It implies that the compensation from firm B to firm A should be equal to - R_1 e_{12}

But it is not a constant sum. It varies with the quantity of production of both firms. It depicts situation of non-separable environmental externality.

The amount of compensation can be examined by checking the allocation rules of the counter players. The marginal principle for labour payments of firm B should include the indirect marginal effects upon firm A. It means:

$$W_2 = \left(p_2 \cdot \frac{\partial V_2}{\partial X_2} + p_1 \cdot \frac{\partial V_1, V_2}{\partial V_2 X_2} \right)$$

$$= e_{x2}.R_2 + e_{x2}.e_{21}.R_1 \qquad \text{... 22}$$

Similarly the marginal principle for capital payment can be:

$$K_2 = \{e_{y2}R_2 + e_{y2}.e_{21}.R_1\} \qquad \text{... 23}$$

There fore the amount of damage inflicted by player B to player A is equal to:

$$M = -e_{x2}\, e_{21}R_1 - e_{y2}e_{21}\, R_1$$

$$= -e_{21}R_1 \qquad \text{... 24}$$

Thus the equilibrium in the market can be ensured by imposing a tax amount of - $e_{21}R_1$ on firm B and by subsidising firm A with the same amount. Therefore the essential factor to be calculated is the e21 in order to find out the appropriate rates of tax and subsidy in the presence of environmental externality.

The problem is how to gauge the compensation to be paid to the victims of environmental pollution. Let us examine the possibility of imposing tax in order to curb the environmental externalities. We are dealing with the problem from a collective point of view. Let us derive some rules for public control of environmental degradation due to private economic activities. Here the purpose is to determine an optimal amount of pollution which ensures a certain environmental quality as well as a reasonable level of welfare. Let us assume that a producer is polluting the air. Its amount of pollution directly varies with its volume of production. i.e.

$$L = f(q), \text{ where: } \partial L / \partial q > 0 \qquad \dots 25$$

Cost of Production of the producer now depends upon the volume of production as well as on investment in pollution abatement, i.e.

$$C = h(Q, A)$$

$$\text{Where: } \partial C / \partial Q > 0 \text{ and } \partial C / \partial A < 0 \qquad \dots 26$$

The producer also undertakes certain amount of new investments creating favourable environmental conditions, like plantation, Public Park etc in order to improve the air quality. This investment directly varies with the amount of pollution it creates, i.e.

$$N = g(L), \text{ where: } \partial N / \partial L > 0 \qquad \dots 27$$

When we measure the social utility of this production activity in monetary terms it is equal to $S_q . Q$, where Sq is the monetary social benefit of a unit of production. Its corresponding social disutility is equal to $S_L . L$, where S_L is the monetary social damage of a unit of pollution. Thus the net contribution of the producer to the social welfare is:

$$Z = S_q.Q - S_L.L - h(Q,A) - g(L) \qquad \dots 28$$

By substituting eq. (18) in (21) we get:

$$Z = S_q. Q - S_L. f(q) - h(Q, f(q)) - g\{f(q)\} \qquad \dots 29$$

So the optimal social welfare is achieved only when the following first order necessary condition is satisfied i.e.

$$\frac{\partial Z}{\partial Q} = S_q - \frac{S_L.\partial f(q)}{\partial Q} - \frac{\partial h\{Q.f(q)\}}{\partial Q} - \frac{\partial q\{f(q)\}}{\partial Q}$$

$$= 0 \qquad \dots 30$$

It implies that the production and pollution attain their optimal level only when marginal social utility of production is equal to the marginal pollution cost plus marginal private production and abatement cost plus marginal investment cost in improving the air quality of the surrounding areas.

So optimality in the private decision is attained only when:

$$S_4 = \frac{\partial h\{Q.f(q)\}}{\partial Q} \qquad \text{... 31}$$

If the Government now imposes a tax t per unit of pollution, then the total private revenue of the producer will decline to the level:

$$R = S_q Q - h(Q, A) - tL$$
$$= S_q Q - h\{Q, f(Q)\} - t\, f(Q) \qquad \text{... 32}$$

Therefore the first order necessary condition for optimal private decision is:

$$\frac{\partial R}{\partial Q} = S_q - \frac{\partial h\{Q.f(Q)\}}{\partial Q} - \frac{\partial qf(Q)}{\partial Q}$$

$$= 0 \qquad \text{... 33}$$

$$S_4 = \frac{\partial h\{Q.f(Q)\}}{\partial Q} + \frac{t\partial f(Q)}{\partial Q} = 0 \qquad \text{... 34}$$

It means the product price has to be equal to the marginal production cost plus marginal pollution tax. Social disutility Viz. $S_{L.}$ L + g(L) caused by pollution can be compensated by imposing tax t so that:

$$\frac{t\partial f(Q)}{\partial Q} = \frac{S_L.\partial f(Q)}{\partial Q} + \frac{\partial q\{f(Q)\}}{\partial Q} \qquad \text{... 35}$$

It implies that the producer should determine its

production volume at such a level where the marginal pollution tax has to be equal to the marginal pollution damage cost plus the public abatement costs. The optimal tax can be computed when the f(Q) and g(L) functions are specified. It constitutes the basis of the polluter pay principle. However, in actual environmental management the most crucial problems that is encountered is the assessment of the pollution damage costs and the pollution abatement costs. In the sphere of public policy the formulation of appropriate rules to control environmental externalities, to reduce pollution and to restore market equilibrium is very complicated. Two broad categories of the controls may be distinguished Viz. Direct controls (eg setting standards of emission) and indirect controls (eg. imposing taxes and giving subsidies). Both these controls attempt to curb the discharge of effluents. Both reduces the over-use of unpriced environmental goods and services. The direct control represent an ultimate. limit to the level and rate of discharges, while indirect taxation policy induces a lower l discharge by imposing a price per unit of pollution. A lower level of emission can be attained either by curtailing the scale of activity or by adopting alternative technologies. In case of effluent charges a cost minimizing producer shall try to compare between three possible effects: (i) total costs due to taxes (ii) total costs due to sales reduction and (iii) additional costs of adopting alternative technology. In case of direct controls of standard setting only latter two effects are relevant for comparison. The emission charges offer more opportunities to compare different strategies of the producers but the apparent folly of the indirect control is that a tax implies a 'right to pollute'. Direct controls system is easier to administer, but the basic problem here is that the levels of standards are to be evaluated against the losses in production and employment. By imposing effluent standards a cost minimising producer is stimulated to discharge the maximum allowable levels of pollutants. But tax imposition stimulates the adoption of new technologies in order to reduce the levels of effluents and minimise the effluent costs. In practice a mixed environmental policy is used Standards are used to limit the total amount of discharges, while charges are used to improve the environmental quality below the acceptable standards by imposing penalties on discharges. The relative share of standards and charges in environmental policies is often codetermined on the basis of best practicable means in which for each economic sector the competitive situation, the spatial dispersion and the weakness of certain individual producer is taken into consideration.

But many types of policy problems are associated with a mixed system. It can be illustrated here .Let us assume that the local or regional government imposes a maximum allowable limit of pollution in addition to a tax system for the remaining pollution. If the pollution standard is L, the social welfare can be revised as:

$$Z = S_q . Q - S_L . f(q) - h\{Q, f(q)\} - g\{f(q)\} \qquad \dots 36$$

Where: $f(Q) \leq L$

Then for attaining the constrained maximum of private revenues the first order conditions from Kuhn - Tucker -Lagrangian function can be obtained here. In order to find out the optimum value of Q the lagrangian function is:

$$N = S_q . Q - h\{Q, f(q)\} - t\, f(q) - \lambda\{f(Q) - L\} \qquad \dots 37$$

Where λ is a non-negative lagrangian multiplier related to the acceptability standard of pollution. The first order condition for a constrained maximum is:

$$S_4 \leq \frac{\partial h\{Q.f(Q)\}}{\partial Q} + \frac{t\partial f(Q)}{\partial Q} - \frac{\partial f(Q)}{\partial Q} \qquad \dots 38$$

$$\lambda\{f(Q) - L\} = 0 \qquad \text{... 39}$$

It (39) shows that a positive value of shadow price λ implies an active pollution constraint. On the contrary if the acceptability standards is not very active (i.e. f(Q) < .L), then λ = 0. The equation (39) shows that in case of an inactive acceptability standard condition (34) is again valid in order to achieve a private optimum.

4.5. SUMMING UP

When the pollution standards is very active then the product price has to be equal to the marginal production costs plus marginal taxes plus the shadow values of marginal pollution. The compensation rules (35) for social disutilities from pollution activity are equally valid here for both active and inactive acceptability standards. When the product prices, marginal production costs and the shadow price of pollution in the equilibrium situation are known, the optimal taxes can be easily estimated for the producer. This idea can be easily extended in different ways by including price elasticities for demand in relation to the internalisation of pollution costs. Finally the environmental management and the tools of environmental control in a country depends on the institutional framework of its economic system.

REFERENCES

Barkley, PW and DW Seckler, Economic Growth and Environmental Decay, Harcourt Brace, New York, 1972

Baumol, WJ and W E Oates, The Theory of Environmental Policy, Prentice hall, Englewood Cliffs, 1975

Buchanan JM and WC stubblebine, Externality, Economics, Vol.29, (pp.371-84), 1962

Edel, M, Economics and the Environment, Prentice hall, Englewoods Cliffs, 1973

Freeman, A M et al Economics of Environmental Policy, Wiley, New York, 1973

Herfindahl, OC and AV Kneese, Economic Theory of Natural resources, Merrill Pub. Co, Columbus, 1974 Maler, KG Environmental Economics, John Hopkins Press, Baltimore, 1974

Marchand, J M and KP Russell, Externality, Liability, Separability and resource Allocation, American economics review, Vol. 63, pp. 611-20, 1975

Meade, J E, The Theory of Economic Externalities, Sijthoff, Leiden, 1973

Mishan, E J, The Costs of Economic Growth, Staples press, London, 1968

Victor PA, Economics of Pollution, Mac Millan, London, 1972

Wolozin H (ed) The Economics of Pollution, General Learning Press, Morristown, 1974.

5
Environment and Population Pressure

Growth of population in the world is unprecedented in the human history. Rapidly growing population in developing countries is likely to put great strain on the resources and natural reserves of the world. Energy elasticity of income is always very high in less developed countries. The rich does not curbs its habit of over consumption. On the contrary the poor can not reduce his habit of using the natural resources as the free rider. The chasm of income inequality is the major cause of environmental deterioration of the globe. In this chapter it is argued that maintenance and preservation of the fragile ecosystem has to be placed ahead of technology, population and growth of National Income

The earth is undergoing a profound transformation with the intervention of the mankind. All human activities necessarily exert a claim on the environment both in the form of input and output. The first claim leads to exhaustion of natural resources, the second one to pollution and environmental degradation. This chapter attempts to provide an insight into the functioning of Ecology of man and highlights the problems of depletion of natural resources and environmental deterioration. It examines the direct and indirect consequences of growth of population, GNP, technological development on the environment and ecosystems. It analyses the unintended consequences of intended economic action in an analytical framework. While analysing the future prospects of the supply of energy and environmental services, it makes out a case for having an ecosystem approach for sustainable development.

Depletion of natural resources broadly refers to the energy crisis. Harnessment of natural resources is a logical necessity without which the existence of mankind is impossible. The use of natural energy is unavoidable in any activity. It plays that role in an Economy which food plays in the biological survival of a living being. Energy consumption is an important parameter of overall economic development of each country. Energy in one form or other enters practically every economic activity and its availability and cost determines the economic prosperity of a nation. There is a close nexus between the Energy policy and environmental standards and ecological problems of the world. One of the major crisis, the world is facing, is that of heavy deforestation. From environmental point of view it is a real disaster. Forest performs irreplaceable ecological services and provides economic products and other facilities. It assists in global cycling of water, oxygen, carbon and nitrogen. It maintains stability in hydrological systems. Thus the formulation of an energy policy is a key clement in maintaining and improving the environment, because the pattern of energy use affects the environment an almost infinite number [21]of ways. Environmental problems refer broadly to the negative influences of human activities on natural environment beyond the sustainable level. There are three types of negative influences[22] material extractions, environmental disturbance by artifacts and other man-made activities and chemical-physical pollution. These distinctive influences can be linked to various types of natural resources (renewable and non-renewable) and. assimilative capacity.

Most important example of common property resource is the waste assimilative capacity of the environment. E and the environment. [23]

5.1. SOMBRE FUTURE SCENARIO

As population keep soaring, the emphasis is on production and growth. Most of the regions have passed through early stages of development. They are now in a period of retrogressive succession, brought about by decadence and an impoverishment of the system. The world ,is becoming standardized. Cities, once distinctive now have a monotonous sameness about them. Now if atoms have become itinerants in the urban- -industrial scene, it is because we have a simplified ecosystem. We are destroying high ~ diversity for maximum productivity and efficiency and in doing so we are creating acute problems for ourselves. Respirations tends to be greater than the production. Like an overgrazed pasture the mature system tends to be destroyed and the ecosystem has tended to regress to a stage from which it may never recover.

It is because of the fact that the politico-economic world has not yet concerned in terms of ecosystems and subtle interdependence in nature. Man ceaselessly strives for riches, for growth and for economic development. He is enslaved to and obsessed by technology and the GNP. This obsession has despoiled the environment and is ruining the capacity of the ecosystem to support life. The land is scarred and eroded, the waters of rivers, lakes and oceans are so contaminated with industrial wastes, that it is nearly unfit for either industrial use or for human consumption. Air is filled with gaseous and particulate pollutants toxic to life. Pesticides used to promote agricultural production and public health has been severely poisoned the environment. Each agent of production and consumption regard their disposal cost as zero and use the environmental sector as long as it permits him to improve his own welfare. He does not have to pay anything to anybody. Environment is still regarded as a common property, each agent acts as if he owns it. The reckless use without paying any heed to the damage inflicted is causing environmental standard unhealthy and detrimental to urban habitat. Environment poisoning is cummulatively reducing the life span and costing lives which is beyond the perception of ordinary people living in the urban-industrial area. So we are coming to a jolting realisation of what have been done to the environment and how we are indeed jeopardizing its future. Obviously the consequences of this vertical growth is ecological disaster.

We have a rude awakening. The inter-action of ecology and economy are being very clear everyday. Ecologically overstressed societies are further impelled to more intensification of pressure on their environment in an effort to survive. For us this is a very dismal outlook, although as the course of events now proceed a true one. With population overcrowding, we can feed them, clothe them and shelter them. But we are going surely to force very many of them to live in niches which are very non-congenial. A review of the past reveals that we have been able to get tremendous amount of energy at relatively low cost. Future costs are going to be much higher however since acquisi- tion of fuel becomes increasingly more expensive as we tend to deplete sources that are easily accessible. Even the reduction of pollution is also becoming costlier. Elimination of the erosion of sulphur dioxide and other pollutants from the exhausts of industrial plants costs enormous for every installation. Such costs are recovered only by shifting along to the consumers of the products, produced by that plant. The future therefore holds even greater restrictions on individual freedom. We can never live as our forefathers lived. Posterity is going to be deprived. Our traditional way of doing things seems like poems of the past.

The matter used to be taken for granted has now become an issue of great concern for the world. The global energy crisis with all its manifestations is largely the result of the myopic vision of the world's past and present political and economic leadership.[24] But -Economists frequently tend to dismiss the doomsday scenario of depletion and pollution with cheerful platitudes. GNP rightly subtracts the depreciation of plants and equipments from overall output of goods and services. But it takes no account of the depreciation of natural capital, such as loss of top soil from erosion, the destruction of forests by acid rain, or depletion of the protective stratosphere ozone layer. As a result the economic accounting system greatly overstates the progress of human civilisation. Failing to reflect the reality it generates environmentally destructive economic policies.[25] On the contrary the biological accounting system is almost non- existent and fragmentary. It does not warn us when the carrying capacity thresholds are crossed. The result of this flawed economic accounting and largely non-existent biological accounting is widespread degradation and destruction of the life support system. An expanding economy based on such an incomplete and defective accounting system is expected to slowly undermine itself and eventually collapsing. .

The finitude of the earth and its resources set the limit to economic growth of both developed and developing countries. The earth does not and can not supply us with an unlimited amount of usable energy, raw materials, foodstuffs, safe dumping grounds for the waste products or even standing room. It is not an inexhaustible cornucopia. It is much more like an inter-planetary vehide[26], where resources must be carefully consumed, waste must be minimised and recycled. This dismal scenario has led many ecologist to believe that unless there is rapid and dramatic change in any governmental policies, the human species may indeed be headed to either oscillatory or declining situations as depicted in Fig. 5.1.

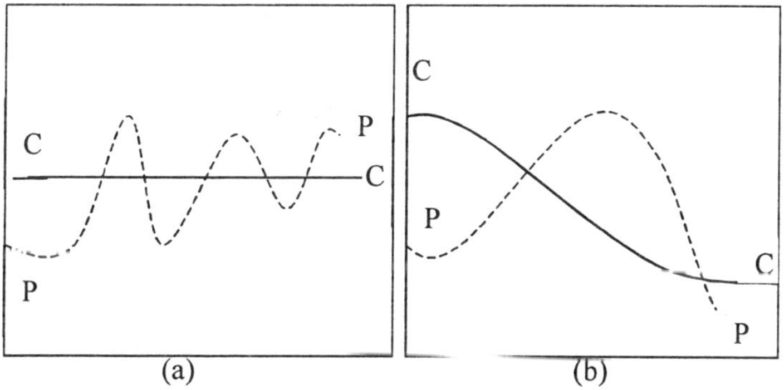

Fig. 5.1. Population and Carrying Capacity

There are number of writings today warning that if humankind does not change its ways some kind of disaster will occur in the future. The implicit and explicit purpose of most of these authors is to help prevent the expected disaster by suggesting changes in human behaviour or policies.

5.2. POPULATION EXPLOSION

Growth of population in the world is unprecedented in the human history. There were about 200 million people in the world by AD 1 and 500 million by 1650. The world reached its first billion in about 1830 and second billion in 1930 (Table 5.1).

Table 5.1. Growth of World Population

	1830	*1930*	*1960*	*1975*	*1998*
World Population (Billion)	1	2	3	4	6
Time gap for additional billion of population	200,000	100	30	12	4

While the world population increased at 2 to 5% per century during the first 15 centuries of the Christian era, the rate at present in some countries is between 3 and 4% per year, very close to the biological maximum.

At present world population is growing at the rate of 176 per minute and 153,542 per day. The UNPF estimates that the world population most likely will reach 10 billion in 2050. But the largest population growth will come from the poorer countries of the world. The population of the developed countries will grow by 17% while population of the less developed countries will grow by 70%.

The persistence of poverty and population growth in developing countries fails to discriminate between the means of production that are environmentally sound and that are not.

Table 5.2. Population Projections

Countries	*Population (mn)*		*%age rise*	*Av. An. % increase*	*% of world ppln. in 2000*
	1975	*2000*			
Developed	1131	1323	17	0.6	21
Developing	2959	5028	70	2.1	79

Source: Seitz, J.L. (1988), *The Politics of Development,* Popular, Bombay, p.20.

Population growth can not continue indefinitely on a finite planet. A rapidly growing population in the developing countries puts a great strain on the resources and natural reserves of these countries. When the population has become too large and its growth has become too rapid, people's use of the countries resources to stay alive tends to prevent the biological natural resources from renewing themselves. The early stages of industrialisation are always more energy intensive. Many experts predict that thc largest increase in demand for oil for remaining part of this century will come from the industrialising third world nations with high population growth. They have expanding population and they have rapidly growing energy needs. Rise in population alone means, even if per capita levels of energy-use maintained, the developing countries will require 60% more energy by the year 2000. This is the most worrying trends for the world.

5.3. ECONOMIC INEQUALITY IN THE WORLD

The chasm of income inequality is a major cause of environmental deterioration in the entire world. The global inequality in income and wealth between rich and poor is gradually becoming more sharpened. In 1960 the richest 20% of the worlds population absorbed 70% of the global income but by 1989, the share of richest 20% rose to nearly 83%. In the meanwhile the ratio of the share of richest fifth to that of poorest fifth has grown from 30 to 1 (1960) to 59 to 1 in 1989. Thus the global disparity of income fosters over consumption at the top of income ladder and persistent poverty at the bottom.

Table 5.3. Global Income Distribution

Year	*Share of income (%)*		*Ratio of riches 20% to Poorest 20%*
	Richest 20%	*Poorest 20%*	
1960	70.2	2.3	30:1
1970	73.9	2.3	32:1
1980	76.3	1.7	45.1
1989	82.7	1.4	59:1

Source: UNDP, Human Development Report, 1992.

Households in the advanced countries, for instance

use as much as 3,000 litres of water a day, which is enough to fin their bath tubs 20 times. Over pumping of water has contributed to the depletion of rivers and aquifers and has destroyed wetlands and many fisheries. Thus an illusion of abundance has led to excessive consumption. On the contrary, nearly one out of every four people in the developing world lack access to a safe supply of drinking water. Per capita energy consumption of the Industrialised Market Economics (IMEs) is much higher than that of developing countries. The per capita energy consumption of US is 256.71 Kwh per day which is 62 times of the per capita energy consumption of India (only 4.08 Kwh per day). Disparities in food consumption is very revealing. As many as 700 million people do not eat enough to live and work at their full potential. The average, African for instance consumes only 87% of the calories needed for a healthy and productive life. Diets in rich countries are heavily laden with animal fats. The meat-intensive diets of the rich usurp a disproportionately large share of earth's agricultural carrying capacity, because producing one kg. of meat necessitates several kg. of grains.

Table 5.4. Per Capita GNP and Energy Consumption 1991

Variables	*IMEs*	*India*
PC GNP ($)	21,050	330
PC Petroleum Consumption (Kg)	2,000	50
PC Energy Consumption (KOE)	5,106	337

Table 5.5. Per Capita Grain Consumption (in Kg.), 1990

Advanced Country	*PCGC (Kg.)*	*Poor Countries*	*PCGC (Kg.)*
Canada	974	India	186
USA	860	Bangladesh	176
USSR	843	Haiti	100
Australia	503	World average	323

If all people in the world would take as much grain as an average American then the global harvest has to rise by 2.6 times which is highly impossible. Thus this iniquitous growth promotes over consumption at the top and worsens the starvation at the bottom. People at the either end of the income spectrum are more likely than those in the middle, to damage the ecological health of the planet. The rich does not reduce his habit of over consumption nor the poor can refrain himself from cutting trees, and over grazing in an attempt to survive from one day to the next.

5.4. ENERGY STARVATION

The rural poor of all developing countries mostly depends on the non-commercial energy sources. The household expenditure of *80%* of rural population is abysmally so low that it is unlikely to purchase anything else other than food. The rural majority is too poor to enter into the market of commercial energy. Therefore, they have no option other than surviving on noncommercial energy sources: firewood dung cake and agricultural wastes etc.[27] The characteristics of non-commercial energy is that it is there for 'gathering' and is available at zero private cost for the villagers. Thus the significant majority of rural population living below or just above the poverty line has not yet crossed the 'fuel-gathering' stage. The worry about the cooking fuel is the most common problem for rural people. Fuel cost is rapidly rising, more so in the villages. It is tending to exceed the cost of food it is cook. It is not what is in the pot, but what is under it, that worries the poor villagers[28]. So cooking fuel in the Indian villages have always been limited to the energy sources available from the immediate environment. As a result firewood is now being consumed more rapidly than it is being re-grown. It results in a vicious circle, which necessitate each family to devote more of its time and labour for searching ever farther away from its home for fuel-wood. As the forests are badly damaged and eliminated entirely, vast areas of topsoil are left exposed to rain, wind and floods. Erosion of topsoil not only contributes to the silting of waterways and eventual flooding downstream, but also accelerates the loss of productivity of land, on which the villagers survive. This effect is further exacerbated by the increasing tendency to burn animal dungs, which is formerly served as a vital soil fertiliser. Thus the depletion of traditional fuel energy and non-affordability of the commercial alternatives worsen the energy-starvation of the poor villagers and simultaneously undermine their capability to produce food for their own subsistence.

Wood has been one of the oldest sources of energy known to and used by the mankind. About half of world's population relies mainly on fuel wood for their cooking and about half of all trees cut down are used for cooking and heating[29]. Such fuel comprises upto 90% of the total energy use in the developing countries. According to the FAG estimates 52% of the world's wood is used as fuel, which constitute 5.7% of the world's total energy supply (Table 6). For developing countries the corresponding percentages are 84% and 24% respectively. In Africa alone these percentages are 90% and 58% respectively. Accordingly to world watch study[30], the composition of energy sources of developing countries is significantly different. Biomass alone constitutes 35% and coal constitutes 25% of the energy use of developing countries (Table 7). The present pattern of biomass use as fuel in the rural households is highly injurious to the ecosystem and has serious ecological consequences. Tropical forests are disappearing at a rate of more than 11 million hectares per year. Worldwide consumption of wood for all purposes has increased from 2.5 bcm in 1976 to 4 bcm in 1994. According to a World Bank report 25 million hectares of new plantation is required by the year 2000 to meet the growing demand for woods. But at the current rate of plantation only 2 million hectares will be possible by 2000.

Table 5.6. Fuelwood Consumption

CountriesT	*otal round wood cons (mn m³)*	*Fuel wood as % of*	
		Total round wood cons	*Total energy cons.*
Developing	1541.8	84.2	24.4
Developed	1252.7	12.3	0.8
World	2794.5	52.0	5.7

Table 5.7. Energy use in Developing Countries

Source	*Share %*
Biomass	35
Oil	26
Coal	25
Natural gas	8
Other renewable	6
Nuclear	<1

There is hardly any national energy policy which is realistic and effective in developing countries. All energy survey reports have remained only as a source of data than as policy tool. All energy prescriptions suffer from great deal of halve enthusiasm.

Many of the gimmicky alternative energy technology/ sources such as windmill, biogas, and many naive and attractive schemes of rural energy fall into the category of *'elitist solution'* to the rural energy crisis. They do neither solve the "energy starvation of the poor in the villages nor make any dent on the energy crisis *of* India". With all our fancy macro-economic models and ugly rural scenario we must immediately realise that the deteriorating ecological system has a logic of its own. Therefore, the success in harnessing renewable energies and new alternative sources on a large scale and an efficient, ecologically safe and environmentally sustainable way which is a technological, economic and social challenge of no small proportion shall usher a solution to the energy starvation in the developing countries. Energy sources that are renewable, decentralised and low-cost must be developed and introduced to the tradition-bound and poor households.

Single renewable energy system is not universally applicable. Therefore, making simplistic international, national *or* state plans for renewable energy is quite an irrelevant exercise. Renewable energy is a very flexible system. Fortunately however renewable energy sources are available in remote and less privileged regions of the rural economy. So one can safely deduce that renewable energy supplies can provide a satisfactory living standard and its use favours the rural development and suits the village people.

Renewable energy planning should constitute an integral part of regional planning. Environmental priorities and potential energy vary with space. The means to bridge the gap between energy requirement and its availability is 'area specific'. So the strategy of energy development has to be related to regional problems and priorities. Hence instead of exercising at the macro-level, the regional planning should have a regional energy planning as a vital component. There is the need for dovetailing the new energy policy with industrial policy, agricultural policy, and regional policies to ensure optimal utilisation of the energy base. The long-term solution to the energy crisis, therefore, lies in developing alternative viable sources of renewable energy. What is needed is to evolve regional policies and measures so that energy conservation and substitution becomes environmentally and economically sound both from regional, sectoral points of view and from the point of view of rural poor. There should be two guiding principles for the development of clean energy technologies that is environmentally sustainable and socially acceptable. The traditional approach to economic problems must be broadened to include all those activities that affect the environment and energy base. An analysis of the capability of the economic system for resolving economic problems of allocating scarce resources to differing and competing ends must include both the flow of natural and environmental resources into the production process and the flow of wastes from the production and consumption activities back to the natural environment. Equally important are the services that consumer directly obtains from the natural environment. The environmental and natural resources directly affect the standard of living or quality of life of people. The welfare of the individual is ultimately dependent upon the viability of life supporting system.

5.5. SUSTAINABLE DEVELOPMENT

Sustainability necessitates the maintenance of the level of well-being so that it improve, but at least never decline through time. Sustainable development path is irreversible and monotonically increasing function. Trends of continuity in economic growth can not be simply assumed. The implication for valuation in sustainable path is quite different, necessarily more stringent than what is implied by consideration of economic efficiency alone. The broad economic system should emphasise on Green GNP which is measured by:

Green GNP = Conventional GNP + Value of environmental services/resources – Cost of environmental damages

$$\text{Green NNP} = \text{GGNP} - d_k - d_n$$

Where: d_k = depreciation in man-made capital and d_n = depreciation on environmental assets. Thus economic development to be judged as sustainable should save more than the sum of asset depreciation and the cost/willingness to pay to avoid environmental damage[31]. Thus sustainability rule is:

$$S > d_k + d_n$$

Where: S = Savings of the economy.

Thus the traditional cost-benefit analysis rule for potential acceptance of any project can be modified as:

$$\sum_t [B_t - C_t - E_t]^{(1+r)^{-t}} > 0$$

Where: r = rate of discount

B_t = non-environmental benefit at time t

C_t = non-environmental cost at time t

E_t = environmental cost (sign will be positive for environmental benefits)

In Fig. 5.2 development path S is sustainable and path E is efficient but non-sustainable. But path N is both non-sustainable and non-survivable, because average level of well-being falls below the minimum level (say poverty line). But from vantage point a in the diagram, it is not possible to ascertain which development path a country is pursuing[32]. Both Sand E look very similar, rather E looks more attractive. Non-survivable path is essentially non-sustainable, but a non-sustainable path can be survivable and efficient in the narrow economic system.

Fig.5.3 illustrates the difference between economic development and sustainable development. So the broader system should deal with environmental, energy and developmental issues together. Our common future now has served a notice that the time has come for a marriage between economy and ecology/so that the Government and people can take responsibility not just for environmental damages but for the policies that cause such damages. The notion of sustainable development calls for

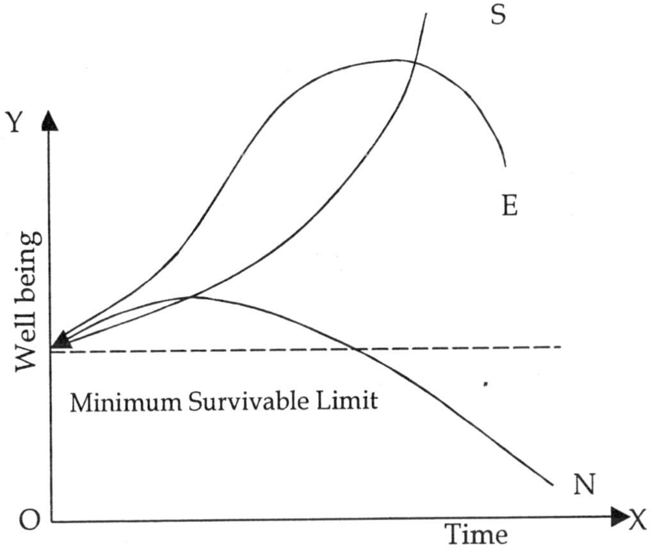

Fig. 5.2 : Sustainable Development Path

drastic changes in our current modes of production, consumption and decision making. It involves the need for a reorientation of our analytical thinking too.

5.6. ECO-SYSTEM APPROACH

Ecologically over stressed society is further impelled to cause more intensification of pressure on its environment in an attempt to survive. Now at least we have a rude awakening and a jolting realisation of what have been done to the natural environment and how man tends to jeopardise its future. The eco-system is tending to regress to a stage from which it may never recover[33]. It is because of the fact that the politico- economic system has not yet concerned in terms of eco-systems and the subtle inter-dependences in nature. Man is ceaselessly striving for riches. He is enslaved to and obsessed by technological advancement and higher GNP. This obsession has despoiled the environment and is tending to ruin the capacity of the eco-system to support life.

Discrete approach is no longer appropriate and must be replaced by an eco-system analysis that considers the man and his coming generations as a part of not apart from the environment. As population keeps soaring, we can feed them, clothe them, and shelter them. But we are going certainly to force very many of them to live in niches which are very non- congenial development adversely affects the environment, which undermines the health and reduces the quality of life. It eventually slows down the process of economic development. On the contrary sustainable development improves and conserves the environment, which encourages the development process. Development with sound environment and ecological balance improves health and quality of life which eventually maintains the sustainable development.

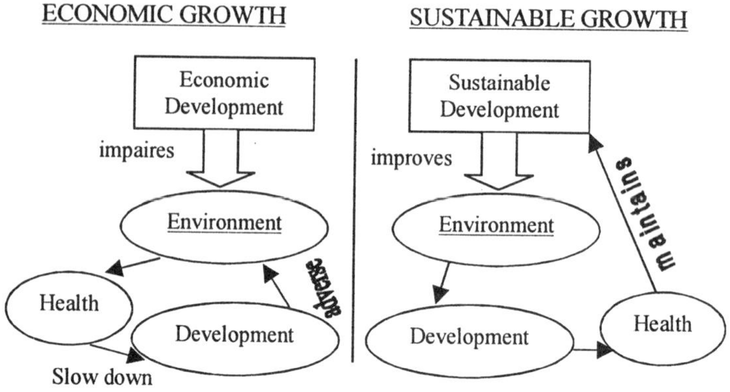

Fig. 5.3. Economic Growth Vs Sustainable Growth

Source: Das, Kumar B., (1993), *Environment and Development Conundrum,* Discovery Pub. House,Delhi p. 207.

The environmental protection and resource conservation and economic development are two sides of the same coin. Development cannot subsist upon a deteriorating resource base. Therefore Development process should be less *"energy-intensive"* and more sensitivc to environmental impacts. No country, no economic agent should be allowed to exploit its comparative economic advantage in *'pollution-intensive'* or *energy-intensive'* goods.

The future, therefore, holds ever greater restrictions. We can never have a living as our grandfather had. Traditional way of doing things seems like dreams or poems of the past. We have to reconcile our demands with the ecological imperatives according to an well ordered plan but certainly not by panicky impoverishment in the face of imminent shortages. What we need to do is to plan against the growth of population, increase in GNP, unlimited dysfunctional growth of urban centres, use of prime agricultural land for urban development and to plan for new cities and rebirth of smaller towns and preservation of irreplaceables[34]. We have to place the maintenance and preservation of the fragile eco-system ahead of technology, population and GNP.

REFERENCES

Barbier, E.I3. (1989), Economics, *Natural* Resources Scarcity *and Development,* Earth Scan, London.

Borelli Peter (1988), Cross *Roads: Environmental Priorities for the Future,* Island Press.

Brown, L.R. (1981), *Building* a *Sustainable Society,* W.W. Norton, New York.

Brown, L.R., et. al. (1993), The *State of the World,* Report of the World Watch Institute on Progress towards a Sustainable Society.

Das Kumar B (1994), *Environmental Impact of Industrialisation in Eastern Ghat,* Ministry of Environment and Forest, Govt. of India, Delhi

—, (1990), Energy and Economic *Development* in *India,* Ashish Pub,Delhi.

—, (1988), Ecosystem Approach, *Indian Journal of Regional Science,* Vol. XX(1).

—, (1990), Intergenerational Approach for Sustainable Development, *Proceedings of 11th International Seminar on Environmental Impact Assessment,* held at University of Aberdeen, August.

—, (1993), *Environment and Development Conundrum,* Discovery Publishing House, New Delhi (ed.).

Goldsmith, E. et. al. (1988), *The Earth Report: The guide* to *global Ecological Issues,* Princeton, Sloan.

Hekstra, C.P. (1989), *Global Warming and Rising Sea Levels,* The Ecologists, Vol. 19(1).

Hussain, M. (1994), *Sustainable Development,* RRH Publishing, New Delhi (ed.).

Kothari, R. (1982), *Environment and Development in Asia and the Pacific: Experiences and Prospects,* UNEP.

Meadows, D.H., et. al. (1972), *The Limits to Growth,* Signet, New York.

Murphy, E.P. (1967), *Governing Nature,* Quadrangle Books, Chicago.

Nijkamp, P., et. ale (1993), Dynamic Modelling for Sustainable Development, *Revue European Des Sociales Science; Vol.* XXXI (96).

Pearce, P. W. and Atkinson, G. (1992), *Measuring Sustainable Development,* CRERGE, University College of London.

Redclift, M. (1987), *Sustainable Development,* Methuen, London.

Sam H. Schurr (1972), *Energy, Economic Growth and the Environment,* John Hopkins University Press (ed.).

Schneider, S.H. (1989), *Global Warming: Are we entering the Green House Country,* Sierra Club, Boon.

6

Displacement and Environment

The ongoing development process has generated an atmosphere of excitement of instant economic growth. In fact all sectors of developing countries seems to be vibrating. But this new economic development pattern poses a great challenge for India. The faceless capital has increased enormously while labour absorption has declined. Industrialization has remain regionally concentrated having very little trickle down effect. It has created the perennial problem of displacement and environmental degradation. Making technology work for the common man is almost an oxymoron. Economic growth per se tend to polarise our societies by concentrating income in the hands of few and narrowing the social opportunities for the poor. This chapter examines the impact of India's industrial development on environment under globalization regime .

Globalization is a global movement of economic integration. Its impact has become all pervasive across the countries. It has generated an atmosphere of excitement of instant economic growth. There is expansion of trade, investment, market, and rise in GNP, productivity, per capita income, FDI , profit, efficiency, salary etc. Within little more than a decade, the word globalization has gone from being a 'catch-all' term used in the economics ,to a term that is now used widely to describe the impact of increased international integration across a wide range of fields .The term *globalisation* refers to "de-bordering" The traditional understanding of the nation state is based on the assumption of a fundamental congruence between a people integrated by strong economic, cultural and historic bonds and *its* state whose main task is to organise and develop this nation. The nation state, visualised through borders provides the all-encompassing unity in which human life finds its place and sense. In the traditional understanding the nation State is seen as the highest form of realisation of a people bound in solidarity. It is the source of all law and the foundation and framework of the national economy. Only through the nation State can the national language, the national literature, the national system of science and arts, the national culture in general realise their full potential. This understanding of the nation State finds its legal basis in the traditional concept of sovereignty. Under international law sovereignty protects the State against foreign interference. The term *globalisation* indicates developments which might undermine this symbiosis.[1]

6.1. GLOBALISATION

The term globalisation was first used mostly by authors who observed the emergence of global markets. But now it goes beyond the phenomenon of the interdependence of states, because it is said to lead to a partial fusion of once separate national realms, in particular the fusion of national economies into a single world economy. However, hardly anyone argues that globalisation in its present form entails a development towards a fully borderless world. Globalisation indicates new dangers which are not confined to a distinct territory. Such dangers extend from climate change to financial crises to globally operating criminal and terrorist groups. Last but not least, the term globalisation stands for the proliferation of international organisations and the expansion of international law, National law is hereby de-nationalised. To the extent national politics reflect democratic processes, globalisation and democracy clash. Globalization endangers democracy in its current form. That endangerment is usually considered to arise "behind the scenes"; it does not intervene directly in the democratic decision-making process. There is increasingly stringent international rules which bind national governments. Realisation of democracy through the supremacy of politics is, consequently, futile in the era of globalisation. With reference to the future of democracy, we have to agree that democracy organised through statal procedures has lost much of its meaning.

Globalization offer opportunities and poses challenges. There is wide range of attitudes toward this phenomenon. It is marked by the end of the bipolar world and the collapse of the traditional axis -North and South. However, fundamental controversy reigns on understanding about globalisation. This is particularly true with respect to globalisation's impact on democracy. The democracy within globalisation encounters a number of most divergent normative responses. The spectrum of pertinent diagnoses ranges from those which identify an extreme danger to democracy to others which find that democracy is undergoing a substantive strengthening. The spectrum of proposals is very divergent. Some recommend the acceptance of a loss of democracy, some call for national self-preservation, some advocate a global democratic federation. By no means, however, has a consensus been reached that international law provides suitable solutions for the critical relationship between democracy and globalisation. By examining two of the main indicators [2] used to indicate economic globalization we find that while openness in trade and FDI has increased in Europe, much of the increase has involved Europeanization rather than globalization. That is, trade and FDI flows by EU countries have been concentrated within Europe rather than flowing strongly into and out of the EU. It is clear from Europe's recent history that the energy behind and enthusiasm for economic integration lies in the drive to create greater political stability in the region through increased political interdependency. Structures within Europe have led to increased openness among European countries, reflecting Europeanization more than globalization. [3] The increasing emphasis in many fora on the need for Europe to become a significant economic and political power block (to counteract the global dominance of the US) is likely to make Europeanization rather than Globalization a priority over the coming decade. Whether such Europeanization promotes the process of Globalization or occurs at its expense, remains an open question.

6.2. GLOBALISATION IN DEVELOPING COUNTRIES

After globalization all sectors of different countries seem to be vibrating with economic buoyancy. The GDP growth in the world has been very impressive. The performance of south Asian countries is better than the high income countries. The recent economic performance of developing economies and the relatively rapid growth projected for these economies over the medium term, owes much to the economic reforms undertaken over the past several years. Improved macroeconomic policies, reflected in lower inflation, trade liberalization,[4] more flexible exchange rate regimes and lower fiscal deficits have reduced uncertainty and improved the overall investment environment. More micro-economic structural reforms, such as privatization and regulatory reform initiatives, have also played a key role. These factors are expected to contribute to better long-term growth performance as compared with past decades. The growth rates of per capita real GDP of different regions are shown in the following Table-1. Consistent with recent improvements in economic performance, per capita incomes in developing countries are projected to grow by 3.5 percent a year, more than twice as fast as the 1.5 percent growth rates recorded during the 1990s. Projected future growth rates are higher than during the 1980s and 1990s in developing region .

Table 6.1 : PER CAPITA REAL GDP GROWTH

Regions	*1980s*	*1990s*	*2001-06*	*2006-15*
East Asia & Pacific	5.8	6.3	6.4	5.3
South Asia	3.3	3.2	4.5	4.2
Developing Countries	0.7	1.5	3.7	3.5
Europe & central Asia	0.9	-1.8	5.0	3.5
World	1.3	1.2	1.5	2.1

Source: World Bank: Prospects for the Global Economy, 2006

6.3. THE PARADIGM SHIFT IN INDIA'S ECONOMIC POLICY

The question of the nature and extent of the openness of the Indian economy has arisen as a result of the opening up of the economy in 1991 and subsequent years following the paradigm shift in economic policy. Of course, it is true that the more prosperous economies today are also more open, but that does not settle the issue of causality as to which is prior. India's decision-makers took the economy on an autarkic course of development in the mid-1950s with the launching of the Second Five-Year Plan (1956- 1961). The subsequent quarter-century was, however, marked by severe economic crises and a low rate of economic growth. Despite the attempt at within-system internal economic liberalisation in the mid-1980s India remained a comprehensively and stringently controlled economy, both internally and externally. Indeed, India was the most autarkic non-communist country in the world till 1991Then, in 1991, India made a decisive shift to a more open and liberal economy, albeit gradually.

Several interpretations have been offered to explain the dramatic change from the economic framework of 1950s. The immediate precipitant of the policy change was, of course, the balance of payments crisis, emanating from both : internal fiscal profligacy and external developments in the Persian Gulf. However, the payments crisis can only explain the policy of economic stabilisation but not that of the major effort at economic restructuring. The new political leadership attributed the failure to achieve rapid growth in India to earlier policy choices, which had resulted in the country's isolation from the world economy and in an overly-regulated national economy. It was needed to integrate Indian economy into the world economy and to dismantle the structures of over-regulation. The circle of people in the government convinced of the need for globalisation and liberalisation and was enthusiastic about reform was, of course, narrow and constituted a rather small group; it consisted primarily of the prime minister, the finance minister, and the commerce minister, and their team of bureaucratic and technocratic advisors. There were opponents in the ruling party as well, who wanted no such thing as liberalisation as it went counter to the socialist tradition of Nehru. However, after a decade of experience with the reforms, economic liberalisation has come under increasing criticism, indeed virulent attack. No doubt the reforms had been subjected to attack from their very initiation; both from the left and the right there had arisen cries about the alleged surrender of national sovereignty to foreign. interests and the international financial institutions, while the trade unions went on intermittent strikes in protest against the reforms. Of course, there are others in the government, business and the financial press, who believe that India has not gone forward far enough on liberalisation, both internally and externally, and want it to move more energetically on the second generation of reforms.

India's position in terms of degree of openness is 117. External openness per se does provide significant opportunities for growth, but it also carries big risks. In any case, external openness by itself does not assure growth unless it is part of a larger strategy for economic growth focusing on investment in physical and human capital and on the provision of appropriate social and political institutions for macroeconomic adjustment and conflict management.

After adopting Structural Adjustment Programme, government of India designed its new industrial policy, which has the following objectives:

a. building progressive economy
b. greater market orientation
c. strengthening private sector
d. dismantling of all controls
e. dispersing of industries
f. redefining the role of public sector
g. controlling of monopoly
h. promoting small scale sector
i. greater autonomy to management
j. disinvestment of shares

6.4. INDUSTRIAL DEVELOPMENT IN INDIA

Industrial output is a component of nominal GDP of a nation. The proliferation of Made in China labels clearly signify the next wave of industrial revolution in the modern era. However, UK still leads the world in factory productivity per labour. India ranks fourteenth worldwide in factory output. -account for 28.4% of the GDP and employ 17% of the total workforce. Economic reforms brought foreign competition, led to privatisation of certain public sector industries (mainly Automobiles + Textiles+ pharmaceutical + IT).The following table shows the place of India in the industrial map of the world.

Table 6.2 : Industrial Production 2005(million USD)

Rank	*Country/ Territory*	*Industry*	*Rank*	*Country/ Territory*	*Industry*
—	World	14,054,400	13	Saudi Arabia	210,056
1	United States	2,643,390	14	India	206,703
2	Japan	1,253,615	15	Mexico	190,005
3	China	973,323	16	Australia	171,573
4	Germa	809,380	17	Netherlands	146,595
5	United Kingdom	591,500	18	Switzerland	127,160
6	Italy	499,104	19	Indonesia	109,158
7	France	453,252	20	Sweden	103,560
8	Canada	304,677	21	Turkey	102,750
9	South Korea	300,771	22	Norway	98,431
10	Spain	300,202	23	Taiwan	97,979
11	Russia	259,245	24	Austria	93,231
12	Brazil	238,606	25	Ireland	89,332

6.5. GROWTH OF PRIVATE SECTOR

India has a mixed economy. Since independence the private sector was assigned with a secondary role to participate in the industrial activity of the country by the government. Only after 6th plan govt started to assign greater responsibility to private sector by allocating 47% of total planned investment. The new industrial policy of 1991 liberalised the private sector considerably. The main changes brought by this new policy include abolishing the system of industrial licensing for all industrial undertakings except for a short list of 18 industries, reducing the list of industries under public sector to 8 as against the 17 industries reserved earlier, inviting private sector participation in PSUs earning higher profit, abolishing the system of pre entry scrutiny of investment decisions of the MRTP companies, removing the asset limit of the MRTP Act, providing automatic permission for foreign technology agreement, removal of mandatory convertibility clause etc. Thus the new policy has assigned a greater role to the private sector by removing restrictions and controls and introduced a liberalised regime for the private sector. Number of private sector enterprises increased in different productive activities. Total capital employed in 150 top private sector large scale companies was aggregated to Rs.73799 crores in 91-92 as compared to Rs.57825 crores in 90-91.The investment in private sector grew by 27.6% The total assets of top five companies(Reliance, Tata Iron and Steel, Tata Engineering, Larsen and Turbo and Grasim industries) has increased significantly. According to to the study of CMIE only 189 companies out of 1664 large companies had 61% of total assets.

Table 6.3 : Industrial Growth in India

Year	*Mining*	*Manufacturing*	*Electricity*	*General*
1981-82	17.7	7.9	10.2	9.3
1985-86	4.1	9.7	8.5	8.7
1990-91	4.5	8.9	7.8	8.3
1995-96	9.7	14.1	8.1	13.0
2000-01	3.6	6.3	4.9	6.0
2004-05	5.1	9.2	6.4	8.6

The above table -3 depicts that industrial outlook during eighties and nineties has improved significantly. The annual growth arte of industrial production which fell to 3.2 % in 1982-83 started improving, finally reached 13% in 1995-96 then declined 8.6 % in 2004-05. During 1990s there was almost industrial stagnation which was resulted by poor performance of mining and manufacturing sectors.

Table 6.4 : Average annual Growth Rates in Production

Industry	*1974-79 (5th Plan)*	*1980-85 (6th Plan)*	*1985-90 (7th Plan)*	*1993-2002*
Basic industries	8.4	8.3	7.4	5.4
Capital goods	5.7	7.1	15.7	6.1
Intermediate goods	4.3	6.2	5.5	7.6
Consumer goods	5.5	6.5	6.6	7.3
a.Durables	6.8	15.2	12.1	12.4
b. Non-durables	5.4	5.3	5.4	5.8

Source: Handbook of Industrial Statistics, Govt of India

Industrial policy involved heavy investments in building up capacity over a wide spectrum of industries. As result over last 4 decades industrial production went up by about five times. making Indian the 10th most industrial country of the world. The industrial structure of has been widely diversified covering broadly the entire range of consumer, intermediate and capital goods. It is observed from the table -4 that the growth of capital goods production has been very impressive. Indian has attained self- sufficient in almost all consumer goods. There has been a structural transformation of Indian industries, with a clear shift in favour of basic and capital goods sector This group of industry accounted for 79 % of productive capital in 1991,as compared to 5% in 1959.During 1980s the share of consumer goods industries like textiles, sugar, paper, tabacco etc declined in terms of productive capital, employment and value-added. The most disquieting features is that the pattern of industrial development that has emerged reflects the structure of effective demand which is determined by the distribution of income. An unduly a large share of resources is absorbed in production which relates directly or indirectly for improving the living standard of higher income groups. The demand of this relatively small section not only for a few visible items of conspicuous consumption but for the outlay on high quality housing and urban amenities superior travel facilities, telephones, computer etc sustain a large part of existing industrial structures. It implies that the further expansion of industrial sector is limited by the narrowness of the market.

6.6. GROWTH OF FDI IN INDIA

There is keen competition among all developing countries to attract foreign direct investment (FDI).This drive to lure investment often extends to the sub national level, with different regional authorities pursuing their own strategies and assembling their own baskets of incentives to attract new investments. The policymakers have used different strategies to attract FDI .

The following table-5 shows the top investing countries in India during the last decade. It is seen that US and Mauritius have larger share in FDI in India.

The following table-6 shows that the share of top sectors attracting FDI approvals in India. The service sector and transport industry attract more FDI approval in India.

The growth of FDI does mean much for the Indian society. Because it has inherent elitist bias. In spite of impressive growth of FDI the private sector has manifested some weaknesses of its own. It is mostly guided by motive of profit maximization ,therefore it has little concern for the national objectives and social priorities. It marches ahead without caring for the interest of the consumers and social welfare. There is too much emphasis on low priority industries having elitist bias like TV, electronic items, cosmetics perfumes etc. This kind of industrialization promotes the fate and fortune of the few skilled and educated people in the society. It s benefit does not

Table 6.5: TOP Investing Countries of FDI Approvals in India (Amount in million)

Countries	2001			2002		
	No. of FDI approvals	Rupees (US $)	% share*	No. of FDI approvals	Rupees (US $)	% share*
USA	589	49,215.3 (1,093.7)	23.50	542	20,511.2 (427.3)	18.55
Mauritius	239	28,925.3 (642.8)	13.81	219	18,466.1 (384.7)	16.70
UK	162	49,942.5 (1,109.8)	23.85	163	18,043.6 (375.9)	16.32
Japan	70	7,352.7 (163.4)	3.51	89	7,408.5 (154.3)	6.70
France	..	..	..	51	6,228.7(129.8)	5.63
Netherlands	97	36,935.7 (820.8)	17.64	..	..	..

Note : *Percentage share worked out after deducting the amount approved on account of ADRs/ GDRs/FCCBs approvals during the year.

percolate to the people or to the rural sector due to the absence of linkage effect of the ancillarization process. It only helps in creating islands of regionally concentrated industries.

6.7. DISPLACEMENT AND RESTTLEMENT

Moving very fast in the ladder economic development does not mean much unless it is sustainable. In neoclassical economics, the efficient allocation of resources depends on the counting and internalization of all costs. But costs in the modern world are not internalized. As a result we get a distorted use of resources that rewards those who exploit the situation by producing the wrong things at the wrong prices and are able to pass on the real costs of running their businesses to the general public .The ongoing "free trade system" of WTO could more tellingly be called the "free ride system", The road to success in global

Table 6.6 : Top Sectors Attracting FDI Approvals In India

Sector	*2001*			*2002*		
	No. of FDI approvals	*Rupees (US $)*	*% share**	*No. of FDI approvals*	*Rupees (US $)*	*% share**
Services Sector (fin. & non-fin.)	94	15,631.1 (347.4)	5.82	108	16,475.1 (343.2)	14.79
Transpor-tation Industry	60	75,839.6 (1,685.3)	28.22	127	14,996.1 (312.4)	13.46
Electrical Equipment (including computer software & electronics)	736	19,812.7 (440.3)	7.37	625	14,172.2 (295.3)	12.72
Telecommu-nications	75	92,654.5 (2,059.0)	34.48	78	11,287.5 (235.2)	10.13
Fermentation Industry	..	..	..	5	7,904.2 (164.7)	7.10
Metallurgical industries	25	9,630.6 (214.0)	3.58	..	..	..

business today is to find a way to pass on as many of your costs as possible to the public. The most profitable companies at this time are those that are most successful at getting someone else to pay the real costs of their doing business. The ongoing mega economic projects like dams, power projects or industries maximize only the profits to the shareholders, while all the other stakeholders are left bearing the costs. Thus the economic reforms can rightly be called Shareholder Protectionism.

Under the powerful influence of the business community, taken privatization-gobalisation on board as their agenda for our common future. Today land grabbing by the private corporate sector, both Indian and of foreign origin, in the name of so called "development" and with the aid of government agencies and state machinery, has become very common. The global capital" is driving governments, including those of the left, to dispossess and displace peasants from agricultural land, even using force to break up peasant resistance. There has been an increase in the number of the landless and small and marginal farmers. To pretend that development can be achieved through corporate-led growth, no matter how high, is to live in a make-believe world. It is tantamount to developmental terrorism in the name of development. The plight of displaced and project-affected persons across the country shows that it is the development pattern, and nature of rehabilitation packages need to be debated. The existing policy appears to be more concerned with protecting the interests of big business rather than the livelihood security of the displaced people.

In India about 60 million people are displaced during last 60 years but only 1/3rd of them resettled . During early phase of development there was Self-reliance Drive. Displacement was primarily due to big dams and large industries. But during later_phase of development there is LPG Drive. It has caused involuntary displacement arising out of Industries, Mining, Highways, Thermal power Plants, Airports, Ports, Urbanization etc. But till today there is no mutually agreeable Rehabilitation and resettlement policy in the country. Displacement results in several types of risks :landlessness, joblessness, homelessness, marginalization, food insecurity, increased morbidity and mortality, loss of ccess to Common property Resources and social disarticulation Rehabilitation package adopted by the project authorities is restorative rather than developmental. Only resting on compensation fails to restore livelihood of the project affected people.

This figure illustrates the cost involved in resettlement. It reveals that cash is not the appropriate means of compensation. Vertical axis represents the asset of the person. The path NR(no resettlement) shows the asset accumulation without development project. This path is distorted by the displacement caused by the industrial project. Person's asset level fall immediately due to displacement.. It remains at a new low level for a further period as economic activity is built up at the new site. If the resettlement package works then new development path is established as R-curve. If R is steeper than NR, then the it implies faster development at time t+n. It satisfies the no-worse of criteria. Then the relocated community is better off than NR after time t+n as a result of the project.

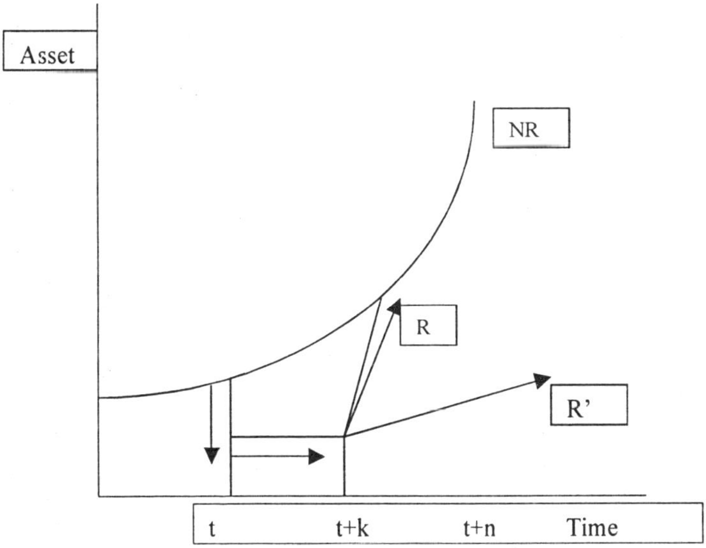

Fig 6.1 : Asset Loss Compensation

Alternatively if the project makes provision only for replacing assets, after the transition period(t to t+k) the development would recommence along R'-path. Then the resettled community would be worse off than the pre-project –scenario. The area L is the income loss caused by dislocation. Project interrupts the development of the community. This income loss compensation should be distinguished from asset-loss compensation. The later involves the replacement of capital assets as they existed at time t. And compensation for asset loss must be at replacement cost not the worth of the asset, If the project make provision for asset compensation then it enables the community to achieve the R-path.

Rehabilitation Policies have their monolithic premises having no perspective. We must confess that problems of resettlement programs of new development projects has multiplied and the seriousness of the problems associated with completed projects continues. Unfortunately the policy makers are myopically limited to economistic alternatives; cash compensation, land for the lost land, Job for the loss of land etc. No one thinks of providing a share in the business by the investors.

Unfortunately the emerging enlightenment has been reversed by the pursuit of 'growth' and 'development' and there is the loss of a sense of human face and compassion. There is 'good governance' versus 'govern-mentality' of state over natural resources and lives of forest residents and peasants. Resettlement should be followed by bold development measures. The resettlement should be a participatory process. We need an approach which should be more humane and an equitable policy on displacement and rehabilitation. Thus the role and compulsions of governments in the age of globalization is indispensable.

6.8. ENVIRONMENTAL DEGRADATION

Industrial development has remained like islands of success. It has not been synergistic. On the other hand it is resulting in environmental degradation due to heavy extraction and emissons. It is due to:

High Population density

Rapid industrialization

Rapid urbanization (mega cities)

Incidence of poverty

Intensive mineral extractions/ exploitation

All these factors have contributed to the environmental imbalance. The whole country suffers from high degree of air pollution, water pollution and varieties of diseases in the industrial clusters. Industries in India are the cause of: increasing extractions, irretrievable loss of biodiversity , energy consumption ever rising Increasing all types of pollution , industrial Waste/ hazards, fresh water acidification, and fall of ground water level.

India has a very low rank in terms of environmental sustainability Index(ESI). The following table depicts that ESI rank of India is 101th, while China is worse than India. Finland has the first rank and US has the 45th in terms of ESI.

Table 6.7: Environmental Sustainability Index

Country	*ESI score*	*ESI rank*	*OECD rank*
India	45.2	101	75*
US	52.9	45	17
UK	50.2	65	20
Japan	57.3	30	12
Thailand	49.7	73	51*
China	38.6	133	104*
Finland	75.1	1	1

6.9. CONCLUDING REMARKS

1. Around the world, globalisation has generated an atmosphere of excitement of instant economic growth. But the industrialisation process has inherent subliminal tendency to manifest the marginalisation

process.

2. There is a disquieting trend in regional disparity in industrial development. Thus with the confluence of economic growth there is a pronounced industrial concentration. Few advanced states are developing very fast. But majority of the backward states are stagnating and becoming the destination and captive market place for the rest of the world.

3. India's most important problem is high unemployment rate. The 'reserve army' of job seekers in India is ever increasing. The capital intensity is ever increasing and labour intensity is ever declining . During the globalisation regime employment elasticity of GDP over the years has fallen almost in all sectors of India except for electricity and mining sector. These sectors which were more employment intensive is gradually turning into labour-displacing sectors.

4. Industrial development has accelerated the process of proletarianization of labour The problems of unemployment and casualisation of jobs, lower wages, part time jobs have manifested themselves in much greater degree. Higher profits has been the result of exploitative efficiency, rather than basing globalization on enlarging growth opportunities for both workers and owners.

5. It is vitally necessary to strengthen the regulatory and promotional role of the state. There is the need for a more fair and inclusive globalisation. Thus far globalisation has helped to create an increasingly global economy, but it has failed to create a global community. With commonly shared goals. The fault does not lie in globalization , but the way it has been managed. The economy is becoming increasingly global, while the social and political institutions of

India largely remain local or regional.

6. The resettlement should be a participatory process. We need an approach which should be more humane and an equitable policy on displacement and rehabilitation. Thus the role and compulsions of governments in the age of globalization is indispensable.

7. India has a very low rank in terms of environmental sustainability Index(ESI).

India should take appropriate steps to reduce industrial pollution and ecological imbalance.

NOTES

1. There is increasingly stringent international rules which bind national governments. The supremacy of the nation State over other societal spheres is substantially eroded, leading to the inability of the State to organise effectively society. Any conception which envisages the realisation of democracy through the supremacy of politics is, consequently, futile and hopeless in the era of globalisation.
2. Two indicators are: i)degree of trade openness =r atio of merchandise trade (the average of imports and exports) to GDP ii) the ratio of the average of inward and outward FDI to GDP
3. The average ratio of intra-EU trade to total-EU trade of approximately 60 per cent for small countries and 50 per cent for large countries (European Commission: 1996), and we make the assumption that only non-EU trade represents globalisation,
4. The average tariffs have fallen from 30 to less than 10 percent since the 1980s

REFERENCES

Ahluwalia, I J (1991) Productivity and Growth in Indina Manufacturing, Oxford Univ.Press Delhi

Bhagwati, J (1993) India in Transition: Freeing the Economy: Oxford ClarendonPress

Chandrasekhar, S(1995) ,Technology Priorities for India's Development: need for restructuring , *Economic Political Weekly*, Oct 28

Das, Kumar B (1993) *Rural Development Through decentralization*, Discovery Pub. House , New Delhi

Gupta, S P (2006)Globalisation, Economic Reforms and Employment Strategy in India, **Academic Foundation, Delhi** , 276 P

Hanumantha Rao, C , B B Bhattacharya , N S Siddharthan (2005) Indian Economy and Society in the Era of Globalisation , **Academic Foundation, Delhi,** 439p

Hashim,S R (1998) Economic Growth and Income Distribution, *Economic and Political Weekly,* March 21-27

Mitra , A (1999) Total Factor Productivity and Technical Efficiency in Indian Industries, Economic and Political weekly, July 31

Kapila , Raj & Uma Kapila (1996) **Understanding India's Economic Reforms , Academic Foundation, Delhi**

Krueger, Anne O (2002) Economic Policy Reforms and the Indian Economy(ed) , University of Chicago Press

Mehta , Pradeep S (2006) A Functional Competition Policy For India, **Academic Foundation, Delhi** ,294p

Nagaraj , R(2006)Aspects of India's Economic Growth and Reforms, **Academic Foundation, Delhi** ,352p

Nayyar, Deepak(ed) (1997) *Industrial Growth and Stagnation*, Oxford University Press New Delhi

Radhakrishna, R. S.K. Rao, S. Mahendra Dev and K. Subbarao (2006) India in a Globalising World, **Academic Foundation, Delhi** , 528p

Rodrik, Dani (2000). 'How Far Will International Economic Integration go?' *Journal of Economic Perspectives*, 14/4: 177-186.

Rangaranjan C (2002) Economic Reforms: Some issues and Concerns, The Indina Economic Journal, Vol.49(2) Dec.

Vaidyanathan, A (2003) India's Economic Reforms and Development, **Academic Foundation, Delhi**

Virmani ,Arvind (2006) Propelling India from Socialist Stagnation to Global Power , **Academic Foundation, Delhi**

7

Renewable Energy and Environment

Energy plays that role in an economy, which 'food' plays in the biological survival of a living being. By explaining connectivity between the energy, environment and economy in this chapter it is argued that in order to contain the rural energy crisis there is the need for formulating a comprehensive rural energy policy. In the context of increasing depletion of conventional energy sources, renewable sources of energy are better viable alternatives The technology in the renewable energy system should be constantly updated through intensive R&D measures.

Energy plays a key role in the evolution of modern civilisation. It enters practically into every economic activity and its availability and cost determines the economic future and prosperity. A country is considered rich not by the amount of mineral or industrial resources it possesses but by its technological ability, it has acquired, and the scientific progress it is making, which depends ultimately in the supply of energy, extent and efficiency in energy consumption pattern[1]

7.1. ENERGY AND ECONOMY

Energy consumption is unavoidable in any activity. The process of production and development cannot proceed without the consumption of some form of energy. Energy and economy of a country are highly intertwined into complex system comprising of many compartments, which are inter-connected (Shown in Fig.1). The figure below illustrates the interaction and inter-dependence between the energy sector with environment, ecology and the economy. Energy plays that role in an economy, which 'food' plays in the biological survival of a living being. Ultimately energy is the means and not the end. The use of energy has a two fold linkage effect with the economy.

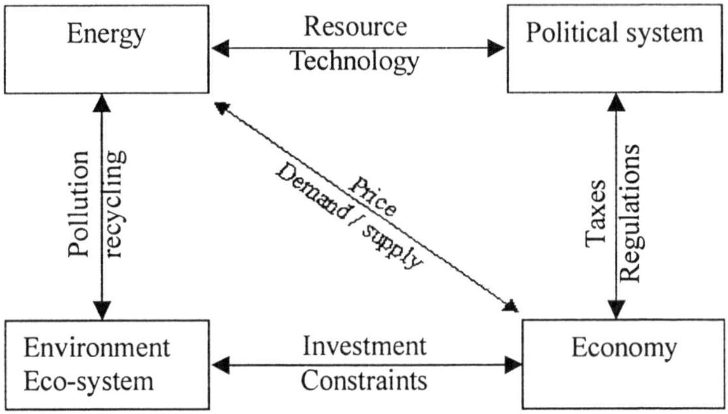

Fig. 7.1: Energy and Economy

(i) The increase in energy consumption necessarily effect a proportional increase in productivity or performance and ensures a steady economic development.

(ii) The cost of energy consumption necessarily puts a burden on the economy and affects the overall performance of the economy.

Relevant literatures on energy are of recent origin.

The issues pertaining to commercial sources of energy attracted the attention of the scholars and policy makers only in the early seventies of this century. Eugene and Scarlot[35] made the first attempt to study global energy crisis, followed by the work of Darmstadter[36] and Putnam[37]. However, these studies broadly analysed the energy problems of the highly developed and industrialised countries. Government of India[38] made a survey of energy sources in 1965. Various studies with much emphasis on fossil fuel and electricity were made in East Africa and South Asia during late sixties. Energy crisis was mainly identified with petroleum crisis in early seventies. The problem of rural energy, however, did not surface significantly in any of these studies. Very few studies are made at examining the rural energy crisis.

7.2. ENERGY IN THE REGIONAL CONTEXT

Here let us look into a very simple model, which describes the need for the development of energy sector, for accelerating rural development. Let total energy requirement of the Region per annum be denoted by 'E'. The per capita energy consumption (e) averaged over one year relates closely to provision of food and manufactured goods.

The total energy requirement of the Regions is:

$$E = e.N. \qquad \ldots (1)$$

Where N represents population of the Region.

Gross Regional Product measures the level of development. Per capita Gross Regional Product denoted as 'g' being a crude measure of standard of living of the region depends upon the energy efficiency parameter denoted by 't'.

$$g = e.t$$

or $$e = g/t \qquad \ldots (2)$$

Where t the efficiency parameter, is a complex and non-linear coefficient itself being a function of many factors. It represents the efficiency of energy transformation into wealth. It should be as large as possible. Obviously unnecessary waste of energy leads to a lower value of 't' than it need be.

Hence substituting (2) in (1)

$$E = (gN/T) \quad \ldots (3)$$

$$Et = gN \quad \ldots (4)$$

Hence rural economic development is possible only with exponential rise in 'g'. Thus with the soaring population at constant efficiency 't' higher 'g' implies higher total energy requirement (E). In other words given growth rate of 'g' cannot even be maintained without (1) new and alternative supplies of energy of (2) without raising 't' – that means without improving the energy transformation process i.e. (efficiency in the energy use).

7.3. ENERGY IN A SECTORAL CONTEXT

Analogously for a given sector, the above logic may be extended.

Let$X$--$_1$ = Volume of production of the ith sector.

R_1 = Total Energy required in ith sector.

E_1 = Energy used per unit of ith product.

$$e_1 = R_1/X_1 \qquad i = 1,2\ldots n$$

$$R_1 = e_1.X_1 \quad \ldots (5)$$

Value added per unit of product, which measures the profitability and economic viability of the sector, depends upon the efficiency parameter 't'. Thus

$$q = e_1 .t_1$$

$$\therefore \quad e = q/t_1 \quad \ldots (6)$$

Substituting (6) in (5) we obtain

$$R_1 = (q/t_1). X_1$$

$$R_1 . t_1 = q.X_1 \qquad \dots (7)$$

The equations 4 and 7 indicate that if the volume of production of a given village or regional unit is to be raised or if value added per unit of production in a given sector is to be stepped up or both then it is required to (i) develop new sources of energy and (ii) improve the efficiency in the energy-use. Hence the critical relationship between energy input and economic development needs no explanation. Above equation explains the raison-detre of law productivity in both agricultural sector and rural-based industrial sector. Thus chief causes of rural poverty and backwardness are:

(i) low level of energy use

(ii) inefficiency in the energy use.

These two factors are largely responsible for resulting low productivity, leading to low income and pervasive poverty. It its rural economic growth is to be accelerated and if living standard and quality of life of rural mass is to be improved by reducing unproductive human (and animal) drudgery and increase in the level of energy consumption and efficiency in the energy use system is the imperative need.

7.4. TYPES OF ENERGY

There are two types of energy, classified on the basis of their source of flow.

(a) Renewable energy

Renewable energy is a type of non-replenishable energy obtained from the continuous or repetitive currents of energy occurring in the natural environment. It passes through the environment as a current or flow, where an internal action is required for extraction and supply for practical purposes, irrespective of their being a man made device to intercept and harness this power. It is also called as 'infinite' or non-conventional energy.

(b) Non-Renewable Energy

It is a type of depletable energy obtained from static stores of energy that remains bound unless released by human interactions. It refers to isolated external, discrete energy potential, where an external action is required to initiate its supply for practical purposes. It is also called 'finite' or conventional energy being commercialised.

These two definitions are portrayed in Fig.7. 2 below, where a comparison can be made.

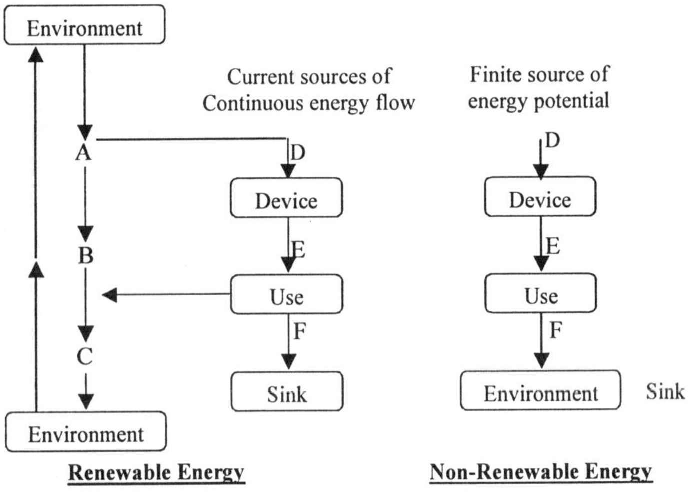

Fig. 7.2 : The Comparison

Renewable energy refers to environmental energy flow A→B→C, whereas non-Renewable energy refers to the harnessed energy flow D→E→F. The former is always extracted from the continuous flow of energy occurring in the environment. This energy is then ultimately returned to the environment, having lesser environmental impact.

Table 7.1 : Comparison between Renewable Energy and Conventional Energy System

	Basis	*Renewable Energy*	*Non-Renewable Energy*
1.	Example	Wind, Solar, Biomas, Tidal, Wave, Hydro-electricity etc.	Coal, Oil, Gas etc.
2.	Source	Natural Local Environment	Concentrated stock
3.	Normal State	A current of energy and income	Static store of energy: a capital
4.	Life time supply	Infinite	Finite
5.	Cost at source	Free	Increasingly expensive
6.	Cost of equipment	High	Moderate
7.	Variation in supply	Fluctuating	Steady
8.	Supply cost	Low	High
9.	Control	Feed Forward	Feedback
10.	Scale	Small	Large
11.	Intensity	Low	High
12.	Safety	Mild local hazards possible in operation	Most dangerous when faulty
13.	Population	Little environmental impact confining the region	Massive environmental pollution: air, water, common and wide spread
14.	Dependence	Encourages self-sufficient system	Encourages system dependent on outside finite source of input
15.	Context	Rural, Decentralised system	Urban, concentrated system
16.	System	Flexible	Rigid system
17.	Base	Broad	Narrow

It is essential that sufficient renewable current is already present in the local environment. It is not good practice to try to create this energy current especially for a particular system. It is obvious that bio-gas production should only be contemplated as a by-product of an animal industry already established, and not vice-versa. The practical implication of this principle is that the local environment has to be monitored and analysed over a long period to establish precisely what energy flows are present. In Fig. 2A→B→C must be assessed before the diverted flow through D→E→F is established.

The end-uses requirement of energy vary with time. If power is provided from a finite (non-renewable) source such as oil, the input can be adjusted in response to the demand. Unused energy is not wasted, but remains with the source. However with renewable energy system not only the end-use vary uncontrollably with time but so too does the natural supply in the environment. The conventional energy is most easily harnessed centrally and is very expensive to distribute, on the contrary the renewable energy is most easily harnessed in dispersed locations and is expensive to concentrate.

7.5. DECENTRALISED RURAL ENERGY POLICY

Rural Energy Crisis has multi-dimensional consequences. While much publicised issues pertain to scarcity of commercial sources of energy like petroleum, electricity, coal, and gas an equally important but heretofore neglected issues pertain to energy requirements of the rural mass. On account of fast deforestation, dwindling supply of firewood and gradual commercialisation, of traditional fuel sources it has become very difficult for the rural people to secure adequate energy supply at a cost which is affordable to them. Rural people especially the poor, women and children are subjected to drudgery of collecting firewood from distant places, spending 3 to 4 hours per day. There is acute scarcity of energy on the one hand and there is huge wastage of available resources due to ignorance and inefficient methods of energy-use on the other. In order to control this colossal misuse of energy, it is necessary to motivate rural people to shift their choice for more fuel-efficient heating and cooking gadgets and to formulate an appropriate rural energy policy which reflects local needs, potential and priorities. In order to formulate a proper rural energy policy it is essential to have a diagnostic probing into the various problems faced by the rural people in respect of fuel for their various uses and to examine various constraining factors in the process of utilising alternative sources of energy in rural areas. In the absence of detailed information on non-commercial energy, animal power, human energy, etc. integrated energy planning is not possible and various rural energy schemes like social forestry, bio-gas plants, improved cooking gadgets etc., may not substantially improve the energy situations and perhaps even result in waste of scarce national resources. It is, therefore, very vital to improve our understanding of the energy utilisation pattern in the rural sector and to explore the implications of these pattern, with regard to various aspects of rural development.

Rural energy problem is area specific as well as time-specific. The nature of the rural energy problem varies from place to place and from time to time. Therefore, we cannot have an uniform rural energy policy, because there is marked variation in inter-regional and inter-temporal situations. So taking the specific needs of the people of the particular area in a particular season, there is need for having a decentralised micro-level approach to the rural energy crisis.

There is substantial variation in the ability of the local and regional environment to supply the energy flow and the suitability of the community to accept such energy system. So no single renewable energy system is universally applicable. Therefore, making simplistic international, national or state plans for renewable energy is quite an irrelevant exercise. Renewable energy is a very flexible system. Unfortunately large urban and industrial societies are not well suited for such intensity, flexibility and fluctuations. Fortunately however, renewable energy sources are available in remote and less privileged regions of the rural economy. So one can safely deduce that renewable energy supplies can provide, a satisfactory living standard (but only if appropriate device exist to harness such energy satisfactorily at lower cost). Hence the use of renewable energy favours the rural development.

Renewable energy planning should constitute an integral part of regional planning. Priorities and environmental potential energy vary with space. The means to bridge the gap between energy requirement and its availability is 'area specific'. So the strategy of energy development has to be related to regional problems and priorities. Hence instead of exercising at the macro-level, regional planning should have a regional energy planning as a vital component. It has to include two vital factors for improving or at least maintaining the social benefit from the energy use:

(1) the harnessment of renewable sources of energy,

(2) the increase in the efficiency of energy-use.

While framing policies for proper and efficient utilisation of available sources of energy, the region requires a long term strategy and for solving the energy problem a change in the composition of energy sources is essential. The long-term needs of the region requires the rational use of existing sources of energy and proper development of the potential sources. The long-term solution to the energy crisis therefore, lies in developing alternative viable sources of renewable energy. What is needed is to evolve regional policies and measures so that energy conservation and substitution becomes economically sound both from regional, sectoral as well as consumers points of view.

In the context of increasing depletion of conventional energy sources, renewable sources of energy are better viable alternatives. The resource base of renewable energy is extremely large. The exploitation of the renewable sources should be the kingpin of our regional energy strategy for the future. Most of the states have now substantial plans directed towards the development propagation and commercialisation of renewable energy. Although the scale of application widely varies, three basic questions have to be posed when one goes to consider any practical application of renewable energy.

(1) How much energy flow is available in the local environment.

(2) For what purposes can be harnessed energy be used.

(3) What is the cost of the energy; Whether relatively cheap or not.

The first two questions mainly concerns much to the engineers, environmentalists and the technocrats, but the third one understandably dominates the mind of the energy consumer and always becomes the final question for practical installation. Renewable energy is likely to be economical only when these two conditions are satisfied:

(1) Distinctive Scientific principles of the specific renewable energy have been properly understood and applied.

(2) Each stage of the energy harnessing process is made efficient in terms of both minimising losses and maximising economic and social benefits.

When these conditions have been met, it is possible to estimate the costs and benefit of a particular scheme and compare these with alternatives for an economic assessment. Failure to understand the distinctive scientific principles for harnessing the renewable energy and failure to have regular cost-benefit analysis will almost certainly lead to poor engineering and uneconomic operation. Every generation process should always follow quantitative and comprehensive assessment of energy-end-use requirement. System efficiency calculation is more revealing and should pinpoint unnecessary losses. In order to contain the rural energy crisis there is need for formulating a comprehensive and integrated rural energy policy. To meet the rural energy problem, it is very important to exploit the locally available renewable sources of energy. Simultaneously the technology in renewable energy system should be constantly undated through intensive R and D efforts. It is equally important to educate the rural mass in energy efficient devices through demonstration.

REFERENCES

Bhata, R. (1976): *Energy and Rural Development in India: Some Issues,* Institute of Economic Growth, New Delhi.

Darmstadter, J. et al (1971): *Energy in the World Economy: A statistical Review of trend in output trade and consumption.* John Hopkin University Press Baltimore.

Das, Kumar B. (1990): *Rural Development through Decentralisation,* Discovery Pub. House, New Delhi.

Guru, D.D. & O. Ahsar (1987): *Energy and Economic Development,* Amar Prakashan, New Delhi.

Mahajan, V.S. (ed)(1983):*Energy Development in India,* Deep & Deep Pub., New Delhi.

Makhijani, A. et al (1975):*Energy and Agriculture in the third World*: Ballinger Pub. Co., Cambridge, Massachusetts.

Manasinghe, M (1983): Third World Energy Policies demand Management and Conservation *Energy Policy,* Vol.II, No.1, March.

Panchauri, R.K.(1977): *Energy and Economic Development in India,* Proager Publisher, New York.

8

Environmental Sustainability of CPR

This chapter deals with common property resources. It attempts to derive the natural growth curve and sustainable yield curve of fish farming. It specifies the fish production function and highlights the issue of efficiency, equity and environmental sustainability. This highlights the presence of technical polarisation prevailing in fish farming. In such a market imperfection the chapter makes out a case for intervention of the public authority to promote economic efficiency of the traditional fishery sector of India.

This chapter high lights the vulnerability of developing countries to water scarcity and projects the declining trend in the fresh water ecosystems around the globe. It depicts the extensive threats to coral reef and other species. It examines the trend of diminishing returns caused by reckless over fishing. In the presence of technical dualism it makes out a case for state intervention to promote the traditional fishery sector of India.

With the obsession for economic development many low income and developing countries have become vulnerable to water scarcity. With the surge in population, global water consumption has risen by six fold between 1900 and 1995 – more than double the rate of population growth. It continues to grow rapidly as agricultural, industrial and domestic demand increases. World's thirst for water is likely to become one of the most pressing resource issues of the 21st century. Globally water supply is abundant but they are unevenly distributed among and within countries. In some areas, water withdrawls are so high that surface water supply is literally shrinking and the ground water reserves are being depleted faster than they can be replenished. This situation has already caused serious water shortages and damaging the aquatic ecosystems. UN assessment of freshwater in 1997 found that one third of the world's population lives in countries experiencing moderate to high water stress. Global water situation will get worse over next thirty years with out major changes and improvements. Industrial water use is predicted to double by 2025 if the current trend persist. Water use in agriculture currently account for about 70 percent of water consumption of the world. It shall rise by 50 t0 100 percent by 2025 as food demand increases.

8.1. WATER SCARCITY

Much of the projected rise in water demand will occur in developing countries. Water pollution adds enormously to the existing problems of water scarcity. It excludes large sources of water from the available water supply. The situation is worse in developing countries. Water scarcity is exacerbated by accelerating contamination of usable water supplies. These countries undergo rapid industrialisation. They are faced with the full range of modern toxic pollution problems.- eutrophication, heavy metals, acidification, persistent organic pollutants. Ironically these countries are still struggling to deal with the old problems of poor water supply and lack of sanitation services. The pollution threat is more serious, as it affects the ground water supplies ,where the purification cost is very high and the dilution of the contamination is very slow.

Ground water reserves provides about 50 percent of the total domestic supplies of UDCs. Mining and manufacturing are the two major sources of ground water contamination. Clean water supplies have diminished. There is competition between expanding urban areas and rural users. Water pricing under imperfect water market has remained a very sensitive issue in UDCs, where most people depend on irrigated agriculture for their living. In China it has been estimated that given amount of water used in industry generates more than 60 times the value of the same water used in agriculture(because 60-75 % of the water never reaches the crop).So better management of water resources is the key to mitigating water scarcities in future and avoiding further damages to aquatic ecosystems. Looming water crises in many regions should be addressed through hard policy decisions that reallocates water to the most economically and socially beneficial. The UDCs suffer from the potentially desperate situation of high water stress with low per capita income. The majority of these regions are found in the arid and semi-arid regions of Asia and Africa. India is highly vulnerable to the water scarcity. The future development of these countries appears severely constrained because they have neither the extra water resources nor financial resources to shift development pattern away from intensive irrigation to other sectors that would create employment and generate income.

8.2. FRESH WATER ECOSYSTEM

While very natural ecosystem is under stress in the world, fresh water ecosystem is the most endangered of all. About 34 percent of the fish species mostly from fresh water are threatened with extinction. Fresh water cosystems are very limited, covering only 1 percent of the earth's surface.But they are highly diverse and contain a disproportionate large number of world's species. In all more than 40 percent of the world's fish and 12 percent of animal species in general reside in freshwater habitat. They live in very restricted areas, therefore they are more vulnerable to disturbances.But they are highly diverse and contain a disproportionate large number of world's species. In all more than 40 percent of the world's fish and 12 percent of animal species in general reside in freshwater habitat. They live in very restricted areas, therefore they are more vulnerable to disturbances.. Fresh water ecosystems face many other risks :

1. Industrial discharges and agricultural and urban runoff.
2. Over fishing plagues many freshwater systems
3. Water diversions for agriculture and urban water supplies
4. Siltation from soil erosion
5. Competition from native and non native species

CORAL REEF

Reefs are an integral part of the livelihood and food supply of human population that live near them It is estimated that about one quarter of the potential fish harvests in developing countries come from coral reefs.Around the globe ,coral reefs are under assault from a multitude of sources. Depending on their location, reefs have been damaged directly through harmful practices such as coral mining, fishing with dynamite or over fishing in general, haphazard coastal development or even careless pleasure diving by the tourists. Reefs have also suffered indirectly from sediment from inland deforestation and removal coastal mangroves from industrial pollution, nutrient pollution contributed by sewage, fertilizers and urban runoffs.

8.3. DIMINISHING RETURNS

World fisheries face a grim forecast. Forty five of increasing fishing pressure have left many major fish stocks depleted or in decline. Despite increasing attention of policy makers and industry representatives, progress towards better management of fish harvest has been slow and the governrnent policies and the market forces behind the trend towards global overfishing remain largely in place. Prior to 50s the problem of over fishing was confined to few regions, such as North Antarctica, the North pacific and Mediterranean sea. With the expansion of global fishing in the 50s the exploitation of global fish stock has followed a predictable pattern ,progressing across the oceans as each region in turn reaches its maximum productivity and then begins to decline. This same boom-and-burst cycle of exploitation has typified the exploitation of other renewable resources from forest to whales. According to FAO's estimate 60 percent of the world's important fish stock are in urgent need of management to rehabilitate them or keep them from being over fished. From fish harvestrecords of 1950-94, it is found that 35 % of most important commercial fish stock a pattern of declining yields and another 25% (showing a steady yield) are being harvested at their biological limit and are vulnerable to decline. The harvest of over exploited fish stocks has dropped 40 % in last decade.

Fish is an important element of the human food supply and fishing is an important factor in global employment. Current harvest trend and fishery conditions put both of these at risk. It accounts for roughly one fifth of all animal protein in the human diet and around I billion people rely on fish as their primary protein sources. Indeed production of fish products is far greater than global production of poultry, beef or pork. However new projections suggests that the contribution of fish to the

Table 8.1 : Overfishing In Different Oceans

SN	Fishing Area	Year of Maximum Harvest	Recent Harvest (000metric ton)	Maximum Harvest (000metric ton)
1	Atlantic North west	1967	1007	2588
2	Antarctic	1971	28	189
3	Atlantic South East	1972	312	962
4	Atlantic WestCentral	1974	162	181
5	Atlantic East Central	1974	320	481
6	Pacific East Central	1975	76	93
7	Atlantic Northeast	1976	4575	5745
8	Pacific North West	1987	5661	6940
9	Pacific north east	1988	2337	2556
10	Atlantic Southwest	1989	967	1000
11	Pacific South west	1990	498	498
12	Pacific South east	1990	459	508
13	Mediterranean	1991	284	284
14	Pacific West central	1991	833	833
15	Indian Ocean, West	1991	822	822
16	Indian Ocean, East	1991	379	379

global food supply is likely to decrease in the next two decades as demand for fish increases

Any shortfall in fish supplies is likely to affect developing nations more than developed nations. Due to the rise in demand and prices of fish, export of fish from UDCs will rise. Local consumption will fall and put fishprotein increasingly out of reach of low income families. Employment with in the fisheries sector is likely to change profoundly especially foe small scale fishers who fish for local market or for subsistence. There are about 10 million fishers world wide. They are losing ground over the past two decades as competition from commercial vessels has grown

8.4. DEGENERATING ECOSYSTEM

Critics believe that effort to assign prices to ecosystem services is fundamentally flawed since these services can never be traded in open market. It can not reflect the full value of these services. There are moral ,ethical and aesthetic reasons to value and protect nature apart from its benefits to humanity. These services are free but valuable. The following table estimates the value of various ecosystem services.

Ecosystems Services

Serial	*Ecosystem services*	*Value (Trillion$)*
1	Soil formation	17.1
2	Recreation	3.0
3	Nutrient Cycling	2.3
4	Water supply	2.3
5	Climate regulation	1.8
6	Habitat	1.4
7	Flood/Storm Protection	1.1
8	Food/Raw Material Prodn	0.8
9	Genetic Resources	0.8
10	Atmospheric gas balance	0.7
11	Pollination	0.4
12	Other services	1.6
	Total Value	**33.3**

Value of ecosystem services is nearly twice the value of the global gross product of US$ 18 trillion Value of these services are likely to increase as these services become more degraded and scarce in future. Indeed economic indicators such as GNP are increasingly recognised as the flawed measures of both economic progress and sustainability, because they do not explicitly account for the degradation of ecological services. For Example: the valuation of the marketable timber ignores the following costs: Soil erosion, nutrient loss ,high flooding, fall in fisheries, fall in water quality, reduced carbon storage capacity, change in regional temperature and rainfall, reduced wildlife habitat, reduced recreational opportunities

Common property resource is that where the ownership is not strictly defined. It encounters the dual problems of development and conservation. Fish is the best example of renewable natural common property resource. It is a significant part of the domestic food supply which earns increasing amount of foreign exchange. Export of fish and fish products has expanded very significantly. Fish farming is an important component of India's rural economy. Inland fisheries including rivers and ponds produce about 35 to 40 percent of the total fish harvest of the country. Fresh water aquaculture belongs to the unorganised traditional sector, which consists of many socio economically weak fishermen and small-scale fish farming units which use traditional methods of fish culture.

Fish farming faces dual problem of conservation and development. Conservation may be defined as an approach to resource management that seeks to leave fish resources relatively untouched. Development on the other hand amounts to the use and modification of fish resources. It may involve transformation of fish resources. It is considered as a renewable resources because with proper management it can be made to yield direct services indefinitely into the future. But its renewability does not imply that it is free from pressing problem of over exploitation and total depletion.

One of the features that distinguishes the fishing industry from other regulated activities is that often there are no strong property rights, and regulation seeks to prevent overexploitation of a common pool resource (CPR). Fishers, in effect, impose costs on each other rather than on consumers, in the absence of regulation. A laboratory experiment was designed to simulate lobbying to influence regulation of a CPR.Results show that competition for fishery earnings weakens the incentive to effectively lobby for regulations that maximise group well-being. More experienced participants believe that their contributions to changing a regulation are not worthwhile. Instead, they focus more on competing for earnings from their use of the CPR. Correcting or mitigating government failure in fisheries might be assisted by the introduction of strong property rights, the devolution of rights and responsibilities to user groups, the use of the cost recovery and sustainable financing mechanisms,

The characteristics of fish resources that make it different from other resources are those that relate to the problems of renewability, ownership and externalities. Despite these difference fish is subject to the operation of price mechanism in the same way as all other resources. So the question that arises here: Can the price system lead to a level of exploitation that will allow the maintenance of a desirable level of stock for the future? All renewable resources including fish are those resources that are subject to a natural rate of growth and therefore are capable of yielding a sustained level of production into the future. The important characteristic of fish is that the rate of its renewal directly depends on the amount of the resource left unharvested. The rate of rise of its population consists of its rate of growth less its mortality rate. The rate of growth of its population F can be considered to be directly proportional to the stock of fish. It gives a straight-line function, which is represented by line ON growth curve. In the absence of any catch fish population will expand exponentially. But expansion is arrested by mortality factors such as food shortage, predation and diseases. It can be assumed that there is a maximum fish population which the environment can support equal to F_m. With lower quantity of fish natural mortality rate is also Low. As fish population increases mortality rate increases at an increasing rate. As the maximum fish quantity is approached food shortages and diseases etc become more important factors which cause high mortality rates. Mortality is represented by OM curve. Therefore the natural rate of growth of fish is obtained by subtracting both the curves. After doing this we get the natural growth curve of fish i.e.NG curve. It is concave downwards. It shows that a sustainable yield can be achieved for any level of fish quantity, provided the rate of harvest does not exceed the rate of change in its population. Sustainable yield therefore refers to the maximum amount that can be harvested from a given stock without decreasing its level in the next period or for future.

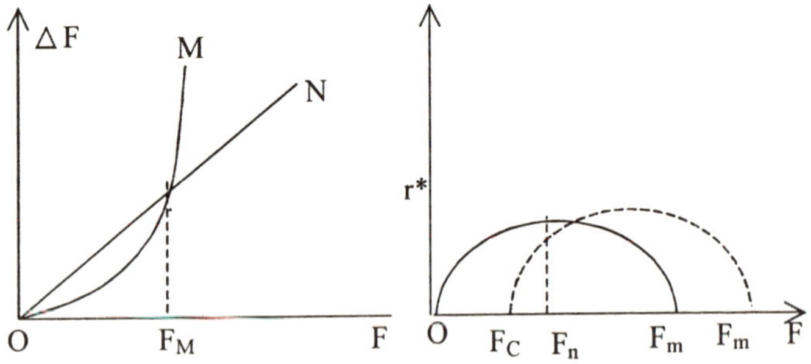

Fig. 8.1: Natural Growth Curve

Fish population increases above zero rate of growth. Its growth reaches maximum level at or* and fish increases to F_n. Beyond that level the rate of growth falls with further rise in fish population. At lower level of fish there is plenty of food and space for their growth. So there is rapid rise in fish stock. With higher fish population the scarcity of food and space force down the rate of growth eventually to zero level at F_m. So ecological restraints automatically impose zero population growth on fish. If the fish resource fails to reproduce itself above the zero level than the natural growth curve will be the dotted curve. Here there is a critical minimum level of fish population below which it disappears .Here the critical minimum level of fish is OF_c below this level fish can not maintain a viable rate of renewal. If man does not exploit any fish resource the natural equilibrium will be Fm which is a stable equilibrium point.

If $F > F_m$

Then ecological restraints will force the species back to Fm level

If $F < F_m$

Then the ecological factors will be conducive to sustain increase upto F_m.

The natural growth curve implies that with proper management policies it should be possible to harvest the resources annually in such a way that is subject to natural fluctuations, a constant level of population is maintained. The economic importance of the **ngc** lies in the fact that it can be used for determining the exact level of harvesting that will allow a sustainable yield and a constant level of population. It is perceived easily by understanding the relationship between growth rate and amount of harvesting of fish.

The fish Production function is denoted as:

$$H_t = f(F_t, E_t)$$

Where: H_t is the harvest level in t time

F_t is the fish stock in t time

E_t is the fishing effort in t time and

$$0 < H < H\,max$$

But it should include another important factor i.e. the stock of the fish which is itself a function of past fish stocks, past fishing effort and past natural growth of fish stock.

So, $$S_t = f(S_{t-1}, H_{t-1}, G_{t-1})$$

Where: H and G are harvesting and growth respectively. Harvesting reduces the stock and growth enhances the stock. When G_t outweighs the H_t stock rises. When H_t outweighs the G_t the stock declines.

So the original fish production function should be revised to include S_t.

Therefore more relevant fish Production function is:

$$H_t = f(F_t, E_t, S_{t-1}, H_{t-1}, G_{t-1})$$

Having the data on these variables one can estimate the fish production function. The results will be quite revealing. A Cobb Douglas production function can be fitted to estimate á and â value. A B values for both modern and traditional sectors can be estimated.

$$VH_T = A\, L_T^{\alpha} K_T^{\beta} D \text{ and}$$

$$VH_M = B\, L_M^{\alpha} K_M^{\beta} E$$

Where: VH_T = Value of harvested fish in the traditional sector

VH_M = value of harvested fish in the modern sector

D = Dummy variable for using or not using mechanised boat in the traditional sector

E = Dummy variable for using or not using propulsion power of the craft in the modern sector

$$F_t = F_{t+1} - F_t$$

$$= f(F_t) - H_t$$

Thus $H_t = f(F_t) - F_t$

So If $H_t > F_t$ Fish resources declines

If $H_t < F_t$ fish resources grows

It simply states that the variation in the level of fish is equal to the growth of fish in period t i.e. $f(F_t)$ minus the amount of harvest (H_t) in period t. So the **ngc** can be used for derivation of a yield curve which help us to determine the optimum level of fish catching.

The relationship between growth rate and level of fish resource and sustainable yield is shown in the following figure 8.2. The fourth quadrant of the figure shows the **ngc** of fish resource. Quadrant III shows the inverse relationship between catch and fish population.i.e.

$$F = f(c)$$

It depicts that when there is more harvesting fish resource declines. As fish catch rises from C_1 to C_2 fish level is reduced from F_1 to F_2. With C_1 level of fishing with higher fish population (F_1) the yield will be Y_1. It implies that fish is virtually unexploited.

The rate of change in population is equivalent to sustainable yield. ie.

$$F = SY$$

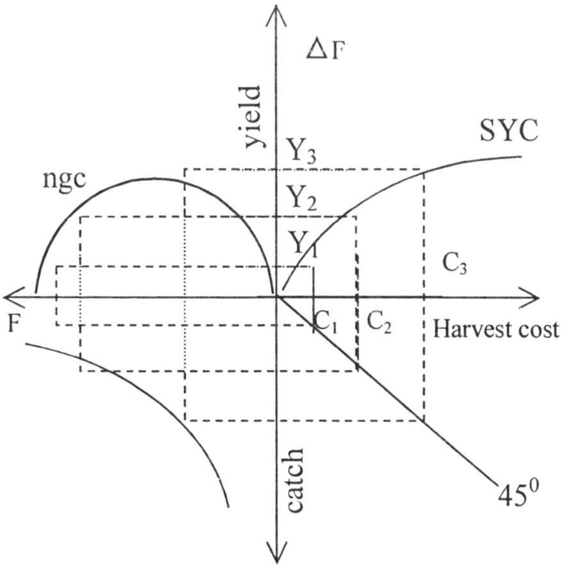

Fig. 8. 2: Sustainable Yield Curve

Therefore C_1 and Y_1 give point g. Similarly with C_2 level of fishing population falls to F_2 and yield becomes Y_2. Therefore C_2 and Y_2 give point s . Similarly C_3 and Y_3 result in point k. By connecting g , s and k one gets a locus ,which is known as sustainable yield curve(SYC). With higher levels of fishing fish population falls and rate of change in fish population rises and thus yield rises. It eventually depresses the sustainable yield.

Harvesting involves money and effort. It has a positive cost. So the level of fish depends on the extent of fishing, which determines the level of cost. The cost curve is OC which shows the total cost with each harvesting drive. When it is superimposed on SYC the optimum level of output is determined. If it is like CPR, which is exploited by large number of individuals there will be externalities. There will be over exploitation of fish resources. The output will rise up to D_3 where average cost will be equal to average yield i.e.

$$AC = AY$$

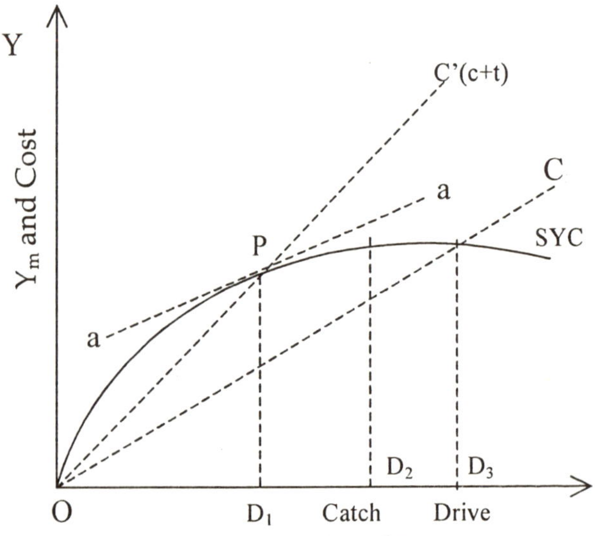

Fig. 8.3 : Over Exploitation of Resources

Harvesting continues till there is profit. But the efficient level of exploitation will be that when marginal cost of fish harvesting is equal to the marginal yield i.e.

$$MC = MY$$

It occurs only at a level of output where the slope of SYC is equal to the slope of total cost curve. Line aa is parallel to OC curve which is tangent to SYC at point P.It implies that at lower level of catch drive D1 MC shown by the slope of total cost curve is equal to the marginal yield represented by the slope of the yield curve. In terms of money marginal yield is same as marginal revenue. It satisfies the necessary condition of profit maximising behaviour of any entrepreneur. From this it is very clear that maximum yield is not the optimum yield. It represents the non-economic solution to the economic question. It suffers from basic economic illiteracy. It results in misallocation of resources. It results in lower standard of living for the fishing community. Therefore economic solution ensures that cost of harvesting drive is taken into consideration. Maximum yield is economically inefficient and unjustified as it entails less earning and less production for each fish operator.

8.5. EFFICIENCY ISSUE

Efficiency means economic efficiency, which includes both technical efficiency and allocative efficiency. It is defined as the maximisation of profit for a given level of input or as the minimisation of cost for a given level of output. Efficiency in marine fishing is commonly measured by the catch per unit of effort. It is estimated in terms of weight, number or value of catch per fishing voyage. Efficiency issues arises from:

a. Inefficiency of traditional method or technology

b. Inefficiency due to under exploitation of deep sea zones

c. Inefficiency due to over exploitation of inshore zones

Marine fisheries are unmanaged involving open access. Every fisher has an incentive to catch as much fish as possible in the present regardless of its implication for the future fish harvest. This behaviour is optimal for the individual fisher but positively detrimental to all when practiced by everyone. This is tragedy of commons. Free riding permits the fisher to enter into physical competition with all other to derive the maximum harvest so long as his average cost is not prohibitive. The consequence is that the fish population is exploited in a reckless manner beyond its regenerative capacity. It causes permanent destruction and depletion of fish resources.

8.6. EQUITY ISSUE

Equity concerns are closely related to that of efficiency, inefficiency and sustainability. Inefficiency and inequity are mixed together in fishing business. Equity problems are exacerbated by asymmetries among users, which creates opportunities for some at the expense of many. The modern sector has a clear edge over the traditional sector. The consequence is higher income and better means of institutional benefits, which in turn ensures continuous access to better technology. The lower income level of the traditional fishermen tends to prevent them from acquiring this improved technology. The existing market structure is also a source of inequality between both sectors. The traditional fishermen are scattered all along the coast and an oligopsonistic market structure prevails. On the other hand the primary market for the modern fisher is concentrated at a single point and is oligopolistic in nature. As a result the modern fishermen obtain better prices for their produce. So measure should be taken by the govt to narrow down the inequalities.

8.7. TECHNOLOGICAL POLARISATION

Technological polarisation is a serious phenomenon in the fishing business. It is closely linked with the issues of efficiency, sustainability and equity. There are two sectors: traditional sector and the modern sector. They represent different ends of a continuum, producing the same product, with different levels of technological sophistication. The traditional sector uses non-mechanised boats while the modern sector uses mechanised crafts. About 90 percent of the fishing boats are non-mechanised. Both the sectors are economically viable at their respective levels of technology. Traditional sector contributes about 60 percent of the total fish production of the country. But the level of income, fishing range, market outlet, employment, social mobility and financial dependence keep traditional fishermen subservient to the economic decisions and operating constraints placed on them by those who buy their product. Because their number is very large and their access to marine water is very limited (due to lack of technical sophistication) So the competition is very cut throat in the inshore waters. The income per person has been declining because of diminishing returns. This technological dualism accentuates the income inequality. This polarisation of fishing sector due to technology is a logical sequel to the developmental efforts undertaken in sixties to promote the fishing industry.

8.8. GOVERNMENTAL INTERVENTION

Without any regulation of the CPR the optimal level of fish harvesting is not achieved and eventually fish is over exploited. In order to curb the over fishing practice several management alternatives can be adopted. The cost of harvesting can be raised by a suitable tax, so that the cost curve shifts. Therefore the equilibrium occurs at an earlier point. It gives optimum level of harvesting drive.

The tax amount will be equal to the external cost involved. A tax on harvesting can also achieve the same result. Govt. could manage the resource and force the operation at optimum level, imposing quotas on harvest or number of operators. Or the public authority can make it similar to any other resource and place it under control of a profit maximising sole ownership who will automatically attempt to operate at the optimum level.

The govt intervention is necessary to deal with the externalities of CPR. Apart from licensing and taxation regulation include the size of catch and limitation on seasons and equipments. These are the methods of internalising externalities involved in CPR. The public authority can regulate in three ways:

1. limiting catches or access by season and areas
2. regulating the kind of effort or technology used
3. controlling the amount of effort by licensing the trawlers or imposing taxes/fees

REFERENCES

Berkes, F.(1985) The Common Property Resources problem and the creation of limited property rights, *The Human Ecology*, Vol 13:187-208.

Jodha, N S.(1986) Common property resources and the rural Poor in dry regions of India, *Economic and Political Weekly* ,21 July 5: 1169-81

Kainath,G S.(1992) Strategy for development of Marine Fishery, *Financial Express* ,4th Jan.

Singh, Kartar (1993) Marine Fishermen Cooperatives in Kerala, Working paper No.40, *Anand, Institute of Rural Management.*

Srivastav, UK and Dharma Reddy (1983), *Fishery Development in India*, Concept Pub, New Delhi

9

Ecosystem Approach for Sustainable Development

This chapter attempts to provide an insight into the functioning of the ecology of man and to highlight the environmental problems facing the world within the conceptual framework of the ecosystem . It deals with the future prospects of supply of energy, water, food, etc. This Chapter makes out a case for adopting ecosystem approach in order to attain sustainable economic development.

Man's obsession with economic growth has despoiled the environmental health. There is direct and indirect consequences of growth of GNP, technological development, population growth on the environment and ecosystems. Ecosystem approach to the resource management is necessary for attaining sustainable development.

9.1. ECOSYSTEM AND ECOLOGY

The word 'ecosystem' comes from two words, "Ecology" and 'Systems". Ecology comes from the Greek word, "o I k o s" meaning households is considered the study of the "economy of nature". The word "Ecosystem" was coined by A.G. Tansley back in 1935. Ecology is the biology of ecosystems. Ecology is the biology of ecosystems. But ecosystem refers to the interaction, interdependence, an orderly working totality of complex factors constituting the total environment.

The natural ecosystem consists of the physical environment, inhabited by plants, animals, each of which in turn modifies the climatic, the hydrological and the nutritional aspect of the environment. Each group of species is made up of individuals, collectively a population, that is held together by some form of social and biological interaction. These interacting men, animals, plants and the environment make up the ecosystem. It functions by maintaining a flow of energy and a cycling of materials, within a structural framework of the environment and vegetation[1]. It is an unit of biological organisation made up of all of the organisms in a specified space interacting with the physical environment so that a flow of energy leads to characteristics tropic structure and material cycles within the system. Inherent in the concept of ecosystem is the idea of stability and homeostatic. Stability implies persistence; the system remains much the way it was. In natural ecosystem this stability means that the system can survive many changes, but still preserve some recognizably similar structure. To effect this stability some homeostatic or feed back is necessary.

9.2. PROCESSES IN THE ECOSYSTEM

The rapidly growing urban decay does not just happen. Our environmental problems and our population problem have not appeared overnight. They have been a long time in the making. Ecosystem functions as a complex of interacting systems involving the living elements and the non-living. Due to early emergence and evolution of man he gradually evolves methods of channelising energy of natural ecosystem into artificial ecosystem to support his own population and animals. His ability to channel energy for his own use changed man's attitude towards the land and environment, fostered the development of urban life and encouraged technology through which man caused disequilibrium in the ecosystem. The ability to increase the carrying capacity of the ecosystem permitted an expansion of the human population, which has reached a level at which it is placing too heavy a demand on the complex systems of the ecosystems and is endangering the human habitat.

The urban ecosystem takes the form it presently has, had in the past, and will have in the future, because of the operation of certain ecosystem processes that permits its growth. There are mainly eight types of ecological processes. Those are: (1) concentration, (2) centralisation, (3) decentralisation, (4) segregation, (5) specialisation, (6) invasion, (7) routinization and (8) succession. These processes need not be discussed seriatim. These are in fact operating in an urbanisation process concurrently perhaps at different rates of speed under different circumstances with one being much more pronounced in its effect than another. Whatever may be the ecological process of work, there are certain background factors like competition and mobility which affect their operation[2]. The competition factor is apparent in all of the processes. Competition for space derives from the fact that two objects cannot occupy the same space at the same time. It may be said that to a large extent the structure of an urban area — the distribution of its population, its land use pattern — is a product of the competitive interaction of different population groups, land uses, functions and institutions. Mobility is a measurable movement in the temporal or spatial framework, specifically the movement of people and goods, land uses and functional areas from one part of a city to another. It is so common to most of the processes that virtually none can be comprehensible unless mobility is considered as a component.

9.3. ECOLOGICAL SUCCESSION

The climax of the invasion process, where the original population group or use pattern is gradually replaced is termed as the ecological succession of the ecosystem. It is defined in terms of 3 parameters, (1) It is an orderly process of community development that is reasonably directions and therefore predictable, (2) It is controlled by the community even though the physical environment determines the pattern, the rate of change and often sets the limit as to how far the development can go, (3) It culminates in a stabilized system in which maximum biomass and symbiotic function between organism are maintained per unit of available energy flow.

The trends expected in the process of ecological succession can be found out by making a contrast between immatured and matured ecosystems.

9.4. THE ENTROPY CONCEPT

For a closed system a situation of disorder is more probable than an ordered situation. The situation of environmental disequilibrium is studied by means of the entropy concept. Entropy criterion is used to study the degree of disorder for the ecosystem where the amount of unavailable energy is ever increasing. Entropy is a very important notion to analyse the situation and development of ecosystem as well as the links between economy and ecology. Entropy is a measure of unavailable energy within a closed thermodynamic system. Unavailable energy is the dissipated energy. Each production process implies the absorption of inputs and generation of outputs. Being a transformation process it leads to a qualitative difference in the material in question. In addition to this economic

Table 9.1 : Matured Ecosystem

	Ecosystem Attributes	*Young Stage*	*Mature Stage*
1.	P-R ratio	w"1	= 1
2.	P-B ratio	High	Low
3.	B-E ratio	Low	High
4.	NCY	High	Low
5.	Food Chain	Linear Predominantly grazing	Weblike, Predominantly detritus
6.	Total Organic material	Small	Large
7.	Niche specification	Broad	Narrow
8.	Production	Quantity	Quality
9.	Internal symbiosis	Under-developed	Developed
10.	Nutrient conservation	Poor	Good
11.	Entropy	High	Low
12.	Stability	Poor	Good
13.	Information	Low	High
14.	Life cycles	Short-simple	Long-complex
15.	Bio-chemical diversity	Low	High
16.	Inorganic nutrients	Extra biotic	Intrabiotic

Note: P – R ratio = gross production/community respiration.
P – B ratio = gross production/standing crop biomass.
B – E ratio = biomas supported/unit energy flow.
NCY = Net Community Yield.

and monetary difference there is a physical difference . Matter and energy enter the transition process in a state of low entropy and comes out of it in a state of high entropy. So this transformation from order to disorder is called the transition process from a state of low entropy to a state of high entropy. So with all economic activity the entropy continuously rises.

The entropic nature of economic processes implies that recycling can not be considered as a simple and final solution to pollution and energy problems. The reason is that recycling process again requires additional amount of scarce low entropy which generally are greater than the decrease in the entropy of what is recycled. So recycling results in a deficit .This may lead to the conclusion that recycling process should not only be evaluated on the basis of direct cost and benefit but also on the basis of the additional amount of scarce energy required . Traditional economics teaches us to recover materials already used only if such a recovering is cheaper than the used of raw materials . It is based upon a narrow monetary evaluation of production activities. This kind of evaluation frequently overlooks the finite stock of natural resources as well as the finite waste assimilative capacity of the environment. So recycling is useful when the external sources of low entropy do exist.

The net result of the complex interaction process of the ecosystem is symbiosis, nutrient conservation, stability, quality, decrease in entropy and an increase in information. The overall strategy is directed towards achieving as large and diverse an organic structure as is feasible within the limits set by the available energy inputs and prevailing physical conditions of existence (soil, water, climate etc.). From the above contrast we infer the following characteristics:

Early Stage	*Matured Stage*
Quantity	Quality
Growth	Stability
Production	Protection
Consumption	Conservation

From the above specifications it is mathematically impossible to obtain a maximum for more than one thing at a time. So one can not have both extremes at the same time and place since all characteristics are desirable in the aggregate. One appropriate solution entails therefore deliberate planning for compartmentalization of the landscape so as to maintain simultaneously high productive and predominantly protective types of separate units. If ecosystem development theory is valid and applicable to the planning, then the so-called multiuse strategy can be adopted through this approach. More emphasis needs to be placed on compartmentalization so that growth type, steady state and intermediate type ecosystem can be linked with urban and industrial areas for mutual benefit. Knowing the transfer coefficients that define the flow of energy and the movement of materials and organisms (including the man) between compartments it is possible to determine through analog – computer manipulation, rational limits for the size and capacity of each compartment. One start for example with a simple model consisting of four compartments of equal area, partitioned according to whether the area is a (a) productive, (b) protective, (c) a compromise between (a+b) or (d) urban-industrial. By continually refining the transfer coefficients on the basis of real world situations and by increasing or decreasing the size and capacity of each compartment through computer simulation it is possible to determine objectively the limits that must eventually be imposed on each compartment in order to maintain regional balances in the exchange of vital energy and of materials. Implementation of this compartmentalization plan requires procedures for landscape zoning which does not work very effectively because the zoning restrictions are too easily overturned by short term economic and population pressures. So zoning requires a whole new order of thinking and greater use of legal measures. So preservation of natural areas is not at all a peripheral luxury for the society but a capital investment from which we expect to derive benefits. It may well be that restrictions in the use of land and water are our only practicable means of avoiding overpopulation and too great an exploitation of resources or both. With human rights, environmental rights are equally vital. The one man-one-vote idea is accepted but more important is one-man-one-acre land' proposition.

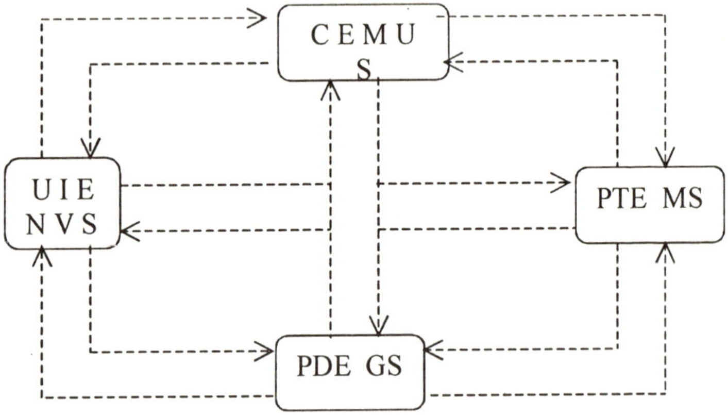

CEMUS - Compromise Environment, Multi-use-system.

UIE NVS - Urban Industrial Environment, Non-vital system.

PDE GS - Productive Environment Growth system.

PTE MS - Protective Environment, Mature system

9.5. THE BIODIVERSITY

Many people may support environmental causes to help preserve the "beauty" of Nature. However, that is in a strange way, not really a justifiable excuse as it is a subjective, human or anthropomorpahsized view. Instead, a logically sound reason based on ecological factors would help show that biodiversity is more important than people realize. A diverse ecosystem is important. **Biodiversity actually boosts ecosystem productivity** where each species, no matter how small, all have an **important role** to play. It is this combination that enables the ecosystem to possess the ability to prevent and recover from a variety of disasters. This is obviously useful for mankind as a larger number of plant species means a greater variety of crops. In addition, a larger number of species of animals ensures that the ecosystem is naturally sustained. And so, while we dominate this planet, we still need to preserve the diversity in wildlife. "At least 40 per cent of the world's economy and 80 per cent of the needs of the poor are derived from biological resources. In addition, the richer the diversity of life, the greater the opportunity for medical discoveries, economic development, and adaptive responses to such new challenges as climate change"(*Convention on Biodiversity web site)*

While there might be "survival of the fittest" within a given species, each species depends on the services provided by other species to ensure survival. It is a type of cooperation based on mutual survival and is often what a "balanced ecosystem" refers to. As an example, consider all the species of animals and organisms involved in a simple field used in agriculture. As summarized Vandana Shiva, the enviromentalist

Crop by products feed the cattle

- Cattle waste feeds the soil that nourish the crops
- Crops, as well as yielding grain also yield straw
  - Straw provides organic matter and fodder
  - Crops are therefore food sources for humans and animals
- Soil organisms also benefit from crops
  - Bacteria feed on the cellulose fibres of straw that farmers return to the soil
  - Amoebas feed on bacteria making lignite fibres available for uptake by plants
  - Algae provide organic matter and serve as natural nitrogen fixers
  - Rodents that bore under the fields aerate the soil

and improve its water-holding capacity

— Spiders, centipedes and insects grind organic matter from the surface soil and leave behind enriched droppings.

— Earthworms contribute to soil fertility

* They provide acreage, drainage and maintain soil structure.

According to Charles Darwin, "It may be doubted whether there are many other animals which have played so important a part in the history of creatures."

The earthworm is like a natural tractor, fertilizer factory and dam, combined! Industrial-farming techniques would deprive these diverse species of food sources instead assault them with chemicals, destroying the rich biodiversity in the soil and with it the basis for the renewal of the soil fertility.

Shiva, a prominent Indian scientist and activist goes on to detail the costs associated with destroying this natural diversity and traditional farming techniques which recognize this, and replacing this with industrial processes which go against the nature of diversity sustainability. Bees provide enormous benefit for the mankind, as another example. As reported by CNN, "One third of all our and food—fruits and vegetables—would not exist without pollinators visiting flowers. But honeybees, the primary species that fertilizes food-producing plants, have suffered dramatic declines in recent years, mostly from afflictions introduced by humans." (May 5, 2000). As described by *National Geographic Wild* in a program called, A Life Among Whales (broadcast June 14, 2008) it noted how a few decades ago, some fishermen campaigned for killing whales because they were apparently threatening the fish supply. A chain of events eventually came full circle and led to a loss of jobs:

- The massive reduction in the local whale population meant the killer whales in that region (that usually preyed on the younger whales) moved to other animals such as seals
- As seal numbers declined, the killer whales targeted otters
- As otter numbers were decimated, the urchins and other targets of otters flourished
- These decimated the kelp forests where many fish larvae grew in relative protection
- The exposed fish larvae were easy pickings for a variety of sea life
- Fishermen's livelihoods were destroyed

But nature can often be surprisingly resilient, often without the need for human interventions.

A healthy biodiversity provides a number of natural services for everyone:

- Ecosystem services, such as
  - — Protection of water resources
  - — Soils formation and protection
  - — Nutrient storage and recycling
  - — Pollution breakdown and absorption
  - — Contribution to climate stability
  - — Maintenance of ecosystems
  - — Recovery from unpredictable events
- Biological resources, such as
  - — Food
  - — Medicinal resources and pharmaceutical drugs
  - — Wood products
  - — Ornamental plants
  - — Breeding stocks, population reservoirs

  - Future resources
  - Diversity in genes, species and ecosystems
- Social benefits, such as
  - Research, education and monitoring
  - Recreation and tourism
  - Cultural values

That is quite a lot of services we get for free. Now, as we erode ecosystems and reduce biodiversity, based on the above list of things we start to lose, the cost of replacing these (if possible) would be extremely expensive. It therefore makes economic and development sense to move towards sustainability.

9.6. DISMAL OUT LOOK

As population keep soaring, the emphasis is on production and growth. Most of the regions have passed through early stages of development. They are now in a period of retrogressive succession, brought about by decadence and an impoverishment of the system. The world is becoming standardized. Cities, once distinctive now have a monotonous sameness about them. Now if atoms have become itinerants in the urban-industrial scene, it is because we have a simplified ecosystem. We are destroying high diversity for maximum productivity and efficiency and in doing so we are creating acute problems for ourselves. Respirations tend to be greater than the production. Like an overgrazed pasture the mature system tends to be destroyed and the ecosystem has tended to regress to a stage from which it may never recover.

It is because of the fact that the politico-economic world has not yet concerned in terms of ecosystems and subtle inter dependence in nature. Man ceaselessly strives for riches, for growth and for economic development. He is enslaved to and obsessed by technology and the G.N.P.

This obsession has despoiled the environment and is ruining the capacity of the ecosystem to support life. The land is scarred and eroded, the waters of rivers, lakes and oceans are so contaminated with industrial wastes, that it is nearly unfit for either industrial use or for human consumption. Air is filled with gaseous and particulate pollutant toxic to life. Pesticides used to promote agricultural production and public health has been severely poisoned the environment. Each agent of production and consumption regard their disposal cost as zero and use the environmental sector as long as it permits him to improve his own welfare. He does not have to pay anything to anybody. Environment is still regarded as a common property, each agent acts as if he owns it. The reckless use without paying any heed to the damage inflicted is causing environmental standard unhealthy and detrimental to urban habitat. Environment poisoning is cumulatively reducing the life span and costing lives, which is beyond the perception of ordinary people living in the urban-industrial area. So we are coming to a jolting realisation of what have been done to the environment and how we are indeed jeopardizing its future. Obviously the consequences of this vertical growth is ecological disaster.

We have a rude awakening. The inter-action of ecology and economy are being very clear every day. Ecologically overstressed societies are further impelled to more intensification of pressure on their environment in an effort to survive. For us this is a very dismal outlook, although as the course of events now proceed a true one. With population overcrowding, we can feed them, clothe them and shelter them. But we are going surely to force very many of them to live in niches which are very non-congenial. A review of the past reveals that we have been able to get tremendous amount of energy at relatively low cost. Future costs are going to be much higher however since acquisition of fuel becomes increasingly more expensive as we tend to deplete sources that are easily accessible*. The future therefore, holds even greater restrictions on individual freedom. We can never live as our forefathers lived. Posterity is bound to be deprived. Our traditional way of doing things seems like poems of the past.

9.7. LOOKING AHEAD

All the while man has been treating the earth as an open system. Natural ecosystem was there to be subdued, to be exploited even to be enjoyed. He was an intruder. But he has infact been operating within a closed system which has been constantly short-circuiting. The earth and its resources, which have been regarded as infinite is now being discovered as finite. And if man has to exist in a finite system, then he has to work with nature's rule under which he has evolved. Therefore, we have to operate within a complex of dynamic interrelated systems of which man is an integral part. The urgent need is to develop an 'ecosystem approach' to the management of resources. Before making the regional policies first the potentialities of natural ecosystem need to be determined. Ultimately an ecosystem approach tends to evolve a change from a consumptive economy to a conservation-economy oriented towards conservation, maintenance of capital stock and recycling of materials. It can only ensure a sound and sustainable balance between a productive environment and a protective environment.

Ecosystem approach is not anti-life. Its fundamental objective is total wellbeing of the society now and in the future. The welfare of the individual is ultimately dependent upon the viability of the life-supporting system. Impoverishment of an ecosystem means impoverishment of the entire society dependent upon it. Thus ecosystem approach is a compassionate concern for the posterity and for the planet as a whole. Mere economic growth is not enough in bringing welfare to the mankind. Man is an organic being, whose total development depends to a large extent on the non-economic socio-logical, psychological factors and on a meaningful sustainable balance between him and his environment in which he lives. There should be an organic growth of the entire environment. The man is only a part of the whole. Therefore, an inter-disciplinary approach or holistic approach in planning is sine qua non for the sustainable development of the economy. Environment and growth are not contradictory or incompatible. Growth if rather a pre-requisite infact for "sustainable development" which is defined as "the progress which seeks to meet the needs and aspirations of the present without compromising the ability of future generation to meet their needs. Sustainable development without any economic disasters, something which neither the environment zealots nor those with development facts even though can progress without contradiction.

Sustainable growth is expected to create the capacity to solve environmental problem. So environmental protection and economic development are two sides of the same coin. Development can not subsist upon a deteriorating environmental resource base. The environment can not be protected when growth does not take into account the costs of environmental destruction. Therefore, development processes should be less energy-intensive and more sensitive to environmental impacts. No country no economic agent should exploit its comparative advantage in "pollution-intensive goods". So we should deal with environmental and developmental issues together. Our common future now has served a notice that the time has come for a marriage of the economy and ecology, so that government and the people can take responsibility not just for environmental damages but for the policies that cause the damages.

One problem-one solution approach is no longer appropriate and must be replaced by an ecosystem analysis that considers man as a part of not apart from the environment. The present scale of ecological research is quite incomplete, inadequate and is still too individualistic to be an effective counter to the lack of balance in the ecosystem. There is thus a great need of studies which can bring about a substantial reorientation of the goals of the society. A solution to the problem of environmental degradation can be achieved through a moral and legal means of mutual coercion, mutually agreed upon by the majority of the people. Permit system, effluent charges, receptors levels, assessment and cost internalising procedures as economic incentives are required for achieving mutually agreed upon coercion.

In a pioneer ecosystem high birth rate, rapid growth rate, high productivity and profit, great exploitation of accessible and unused resources are advantageous but as the saturation level approaches, these drives must be shifted to the consideration of symbiosis, birth control, and the recycling of resources. A balance between the youth and maturity in the socio-environmental system therefore should be the basic goal, if man as a species is to successfully pass through the present rapid growth stage to which he is well-adapted to the eventual equilibrium density stage of which he as yet has little understanding and to which he shows little tendency to adapt. So efforts are essential if we are to maintain any resemblance of the standard of living that has been attained already. We have to reconcile our demand with the need (ecological imperatives) according to an well order plan but not by panicky of impoverishment in the face of imminent shortages. What we need to do is to plan against the increase in population, increase in GDP, unlimited dysfunctional growth of cities, use of prime agricultural land for urban development and to plan for new cities, and rebirth of smaller towns and preservation of irreplaceable. We have to place the maintenance and preservation of the fragile ecosystem ahead of technology, population and economic growth.

REFERENCES

1. Bates Martson (1960) *The Forest and the Sea*, Random House, New York.
2. Breese, Gerald (1978) *Urbanisation in newly Developing Countries.*
3. Dasmann, R (1968) *A different kind of country*, Macmillan, New York.
4. Donella H. Meadows, et. al (1972) *The Limits to Growth*, Universe Books for Potomal Associates, New York.
5. Dubos Rene (1968) *Human and Animal,* Scribner, New York.
6. Gadgil, M (1985) Towards an Ecological History of India: *Economic and Political Weekly,* Vol. XX, No.45-47 special No.pp.1909-18.
7. Hardin, G. (1968) *Science*, 162: p.1243.
8. Murphy, E.P. (1967), *Governing Nature,* Quadrangle Books, Chicago.
9. Odum, E.P. (1976) The strategy of Ecosystem development in the *Ecology of man*(ed) Robert Leo Smith, Section-III, Harper and Row
10. Ridkar, R.K. (1973) To grow or Not to grow – that's the Relevant Question, *Science*, 182 pp.1315-18.
11. Smith, R.L. (1976) (ed). *The Ecology of man an ecosystem approach*, Harper & Row.
12. Tansley, A.G. (1935) The use and Abuse of Vegetational Concepts and terms, *Ecology* 16:284-307.

10
Natural Disasters and Environment

The public authority suffers from inaccurate understanding about natural calamities and their consequences and remedies. With hasty understanding, we respond very randomly to post disaster crisis. Each natural disaster destroys the biodiversity and contributes to environmental imbalance. An integrated development of disaster affected areas has the real danger of floundering on tile rock of departmentalism. Hence to overcome these problems it is imperative to devise an organisational and managerial innovations with in a sound functional framework.

Natural disasters refers to the catastrophic situation in which day to day pattern of life on the earth are suddenly disrupted and people are plunged into helplessness and sufferings. Natural calamities[39] occur in all countries of the world. But the frequency and intensity of all disasters in the third world countries is very high. The gravity of the problem associated with each type of disaster and with each region significantly differs. But the public authority suffers from inaccurate understanding about natural calamities and their consequences and remedies, be it Bhuj-Koch quake, Latuer's quake, Orissa's super cyclone,

Andhra's super flood or Kalahandi's drought or Bhopal gas tragedy. Two third of world's population live in developing countries and ninety five percent of disaster related deaths occur in these countries. Among all continents 87 percent of deaths have occurred due to disasters in Asia alone. Earthquake, Typhoon, cyclones, hurricanes and Tornadoes together account for 70 percent of all disaster related deaths in India. The annual average number of people killed and affected by various kinds of natural disasters is always increasing. The Asian scenario is worsening continually[40]. It is revealed from the following table 10.1.

Table 10.1 No of People died and Affected

Annual Average Number of People killed (1972-96)	*World*	*Asia*	*India(1987-96)*
Killed	136,790	46,353	5,063
Affected	143512,164	126092,412	56563,631

Every natural calamity, though varying in its cause, frequency, predictability, impact, duration and controllability rolls back the economic growth. Sometimes people's actions responses to natural disasters tend to be careless, spontaneous, unplanned and uncoordinated, which leads to further man made crises. Generally the coping capacity to these calamities is more in advanced countries than in the underdeveloped countries. A large portion of world's natural disasters is experienced in poor regions, which are badly equipped to deal with such events. This results in substantial loss of life, social upheaval in the first instance and destruction and disruption of vital production and communication in the second instance[41]. It is estimated that the material value of losses in these countries exceeds the annual increase in GNP, thus retarding the development or even resulting in negative economic growth, despite substantial aid currently being given by advanced industrialised nations to developing countries for disaster relief.

10.1. CRUELTY OF THE NATURE

In India, eight states: Orissa, West Bengal, Andhra, Tamilnadu, Karnatak, Maharastra and Gujrat are more cyclones prone, flood prone and quake prone states. It is irony to observe that disaster prone areas have been high-density centers of population. So all these disasters have tended to be more destructive by affecting ever-larger concentration of population. The aftermath effects of these disasters should be viewed not only in humanitarian and broad social terms but also in terms of economic terms since it is indeed a formidable obstacle to economic development of the region. One should be concerned with the effects on the population they afflict. We should examine the demographic and environmental consequences of such crises in terms, for example, of their effect on morbidity, mortality, fertility, migration as well as their impact on social, economic and political structures.

India has such diversity that one can form contrary opinion about its hydrological conditions and ecological characteristics. When drought occurs in KBK districts regularly a feeling that nature has been too niggardly in the matter of water endowment comes to many of us. As news of flood havoc in almost every year in the coastal districts, with the excessive rainfall pours in, we begin feeling a sense of tyranny of our water bounty. In between these fluctuating moods, one gets really baffled. Unfortunately India has suffered from simultaneous occurrence of drought, flood and earthquake with in one year. One tends to believe in Malthusian theory of population.

10.2. ORISSA' SUPER CYCLONE

Cyclone is the most menancing natural calamity,

which haunts the Indian peninsula and repeats every few years. In the state of Orissa, which belongs to the eastern part of India, constitutes the coastal belt of Bay of Bengal. It is the poorest and most backward region of the country. In this region it is observed that from prehistoric time flood plains, adjoining the banks of rivers and cyclone prone areas have been high-density centers of rural population. So all types of natural calamities such as flood, cyclone and droughts are annual recurring phenomena in this state. So all these disasters have tended to be more destructive by affecting ever larger concentration of population Orissa has such diversity that one can form contrary opinion about its hydrological conditions and ecological characteristics. When drought occurs in KBK districts regularly a feeling that nature has been too niggardly in the matter of water endowment comes to many of us. As news of flood havoc in almost every year in the coastal districts, with the excessive rainfall pours in, we begin feeling a sense of tyranny of our water bounty. In between these fluctuating moods, one gets baffled by seemingly paradoxical phenomenon of simultaneous occurrence of drought and flood in the same calendar year.

The aftermath effects of these disasters should be viewed not only in humanitarian and broad social terms but also in terms of economic terms since it is indeed a formidable obstacle to economic development of the region. One should be concerned with the effects on the population they afflict. We should examine the demographic consequences of such crises in terms, for example, of their effect on morbidity, mortality, fertility, migration as well as their impact on social, economic and political structures.

a. Rural Life

The recent super cyclone, which followed the cyclone occurred in Ganjam district of Orissa just three weeks before, is the greatest horrendous event of the century in the country. It has tormentingly affected three major undivided districts of Orissa: Cuttack,Balasore and Puri. These four districts having long coastal lines are most vulnerable to cyclones and floods. Unfortunately the economic development of Orissa is based on the prosperity of the coastal districts, which are most susceptible to natural calamities. The recent cyclone, which occurred on 29th October, continued for more than 40 hours with speed of 300 km per hour. The sea roared like missiles. Cries of the helpless victims rent the air as the entire coastal belt of Orissa was devastated by the furious wind. Villages have become homeless and towns have become trees less. Nature is crueler than one perceives. The situation has become grimmer as the ninety percent of the cyclone-affected area were marooned under the floodwater. The flash of flood in Baitarani, Salandi, Subernarekha, Budhanalanga, Kusei and Kharasrotta triggered by heavy rainfall have rendered thousands of people in Jajpur, Kendrapara,Bhadrak, Balasore and Jagatsinghpur districts homeless. Hunger among the people has overtaken all emotions. In some villages none is left to shed tears. Entire atmosphere after the cyclone has become cool and calm. Even vultures and crows are absent to fight with the dogs eating the dead bodies. Being rendered homeless by the storm, lakhs of people are on the road. They have taken shelter in the roofless schools, wall less village clubs,open puja pendals or in neighbour's small (2-3 room) bulidings, which are very rare and which have accomodated hundreds of people in the cyclone night with out having any distinction between rich and poor, friend and enemy, male and female and brahmin and harijan. They eat and sleep together. Some cases it is found that people have spent two nights with the most poisonous snakes and furious animals under the same roof. It is also found that houses are washed away by flood where the small innocent orphan baby of two years old has survived innocently siting on the thatched roof eating a ripe palm .In a village of 350 members only one lady is alive who had gone to her father's place.[42]

The scene of devastation and cries of victims is not easily one believable, unless one sees in own eye. No description will be adequate to depict the real story. They hopelessly lie tired, looking to the sky and counting the number of helicopters flying over their village every day. Some Villages have become completely inaccessible. It is even difficult to reach some villages even by bicycle because of flood. People used to move from one house to another with the help of floating buoy of bannana trees. There is no land or space as a result male person used to climb trees to make toilet. There are no radio or television or newspapers. People enjoy the fast moving rumours regarding everything. There is common kitchen cooking one meal a day (Bhat and dalma, or khechri). There is no fuel to cook that bare rice or boil the contaminated water. Even they consider their own relatives rushing from Bombay, Calcutta, Surat to see them as outsiders[43]. Perhaps they have to continue with this situation for some more weeks till they reconstruct their houses and till they overcome the psychological trauma.

b. Urban Life

In the towns electricity, water and telephone services are completely disrupted for more than 10 days. Roads could not be cleared for 5 days in Capital City. People have to trek to different places to fetch drinking water. Town suffered from water logging and contaminated rainwater. Drain water of waist high entered into the first floor of building of Cuttack town. Syntax water tanks were blown off like baloons in Bhubaneswar City. The life of slum people is beyond any description. Dead pigs and bloated cows float in front of the meal they take. They have no choice. They are devoting time to cyclone related activities. They do not repair the repairables in the hope of getting some relief aid from the public authority. They have remained neglected for more than 15 days. As a result they suffer for several weeks with out having a roof. All massive trees are uprooted. The imagination of the town dwellers about the incidence of sunstroke this coming summer make them more panick. Schools and colleges in the town areas have not started functioning even after 20 days of the cyclone. Rural situation is still worse.

c . Relief Operations

Though Orissa has been facing cyclones and floods regularly, unfortunately over the years the building materials, techniques, housing structures in the villages, roads, electricity connections have evolved into such forms, which are completely unsuited to withstand a flood or cyclone. In the recent cyclone people of the affected districts were no way prepared and alert. They are always careless to the warnings because, the predictions of meteorological Department in the past were either wrong or partially true. The devastation both physical and psychological is enormous. Relief poured in promptly from all over the country. The quick provisions of temporary shelter, food for the victims of the motorable villages is by and large a success story. But many inaccessive villages have remained unattended for more than 20 days. Army has now been successful to open roads till Antapur ,Goda and Balitutha and relief materials have reached some of the interior villages. Army has escorted 383 and 300 trucks of relief materials to Jagatsinhpur and Kendrapara districts repectively. It has unloaded 454 trucks of food material from the naval ship at Paradeep port for distribution.

Though this disaster is the unprecedented event it is not yet declared as national calamity. The damages of

Latuer earthquate, Jabalpur earthquake, flood in UP, Bihar, Gujrat were declared as national calamities even though the damage had been much less as compared to the recent Orissa's super cyclone[6] Every minister and central authorities say that there is "no dearth of funds" for undertaking relief measures. Relief materials are pouring everyday from different parts and different sources of the country and abroad.

Despite loud claims by the state Govt. of establishing road links to all parts of the cyclone ravaged districts and supplying of relief materials to all affected people, relief is yet to reach the majority of the real needy. All that they have received after 20 days of the cyclone a few packets of food. Now the villagers are crawling out of their collapsed houses and begging for a blanket or a piece of polythene. They lay down their children on the roads as a part of their begging tactics. The Govt. is complacent and says, "we have done our best. No body should expect wonders from the Govt. faced with disaster of such a magnitude" The Govt. of Andhra Pradesh become 'the friend in need is friend indeed' with very swift and vigorous action just few hours after the cyclone. Madhya Pradesh Govt has adopted Jajpur District for reconstruction. They intend to take up the reconstruction of schools, hospitals, bridges and culverts on a priority basis. Punjab has adopted Jagatsingpur district for relief and reconstruction works. Arunanchal Pradesh has adopted Mayurbhanj district for rehabilitation. Tamilnadu has adopted Kendrapara district. After the construction of kutcha roads by the Indian army some voluntary agencies and media persons got in touch with the hapless survivors and now have started operating. They are disposing the dead bodies and carcasses. Some have started free kitchens at many places. Even some people have to walk for more than six to seven km and stand in a long queue to get one meal for the whole day. Punjabi langar has made a massive arrangement to feed one lakh starving mouths everyday in Jagatsinghpur district. But question is what will happen once relief operation ceases after few days.

The state administration has unveiled an economic package for cyclone affected people. It includes supply of BPL (below poverty line) rice for five months, 50 percent subsidy on supply of agricultural seeds to the farmers in the affected areas. There are plans to waive loan upto Rs.5000. and provide interest free loans of Rs.25000 to each affected family. There is plan to provide crop insurance to the non-insured farmers. There is plan for housing subsidy and soft loan to be given by HUDCO. There is plan for exempting sales taxes on edible oil, pulses and seeds etc Housing Subsidy: The state Govt. has proposed to cover all affected families in the below poverty line (BPL) categories under housing reconstruction scheme, previously known as Indira Awas Yojana.

d. Law and Order

It is saddening to observe the scene of continuous looting on the highways after the cyclone. They are not the hungry people nor for the later. They are not the real homeless ravaged people. Many of them are local holigans, gundas, dadas trying to exploit the situation to their personal benefit. Now they got the nice opportunity of stylising themselves as the patriotic leaders of the locality. They are the group who sometimes guide and misguide the outside relief teams. All the trees are cut and stolen by the private people. They also cut the unaffected trees and carry the log of woods to their home. Electric polls, wires and telephone lines are stolen away. And the criminal silence of the state administration has generated a feeling of insecurity everywhere. It will result in acute shortage of food items, inducing inflationary pressure. The common man will ultimately suffer from the lawlessness syndrome.

e. Bovine Economy

More than Fifty percent of the livestock population, which was an important source of income in the cyclone-hit districts are dead[8]. The situation that now prevails for animal husbandry is very alarming. Govt. machinery is busy in relief operation but the livestock population is facing starvation following acute shortage of food, fodder and water. The Govt. department has no stock of cattle feed for lakhs of buffalos and other livestocks, which survived the cyclone. They are left at God's mercy. Many of them are suffering from fever and dehydration after consuming the polluted water. It has become another source of worries for the village people.

f. Health Services

Stench emanating from bloated bodies, decomposed beyond recognition and animal carcasses makes the situation worse. Death toll is ever increasing.[9] Inflow of patients in the hospitals are ever increasing. Earthmovers and dumpers are used to remove the dead bodies of man and animal together. Missionaries, NGOs and State administration has prepared for a mass burial in Paradep,Cuttack and Kendrapara towns, five days after the killer cyclone left a devastating trail.There are many cases of death due to cholera and diarrheal disorder. With the slight trepidation of risk, volunteers and personnel of missionary organisation have entered into the villages, as they have not taken any vaccine. Samples are collected by a team of national Institute of Communicable diseases from Ersama, Balikuda, Mahakalpara and Kujanga blocks and examined by ICMR, New Delhi and tested Cholera positive. Health teams from other states like, Andhra, Punjab, Maharastra and Madhya Pradesh are also helping the health administration in different areas. There is no complacency in the rural health services. Lack of desanitisation measures and water purification may cause severe health hazards in the towns. Plight of poor people and patients in the hospital seems to be getting worse by each passing day. Being hopeless some patients are leaving the hospital and going back to their homeless villages by keeping faith on "lord Jaganath".

10.3. ENVIRONMENTAL EFFECTS

The state of Orissa suffers from environmental imbalance like floods and droughts, because of the expansion of rain shadow zones and denudation of large forest patch. When drought has devastated western Orissa, cyclone and flood have not spared the well off coastal districts of the state. The increasing frequency and intensity of the continual onslaughts have made the environmentalists more concerned. The systematic falling of trees has first sent the warning signals and then wrecked havoc. Dense forest of coastal belt has been plagued by the rain shadow phenomenon. The virgin and rich mangroves forest is being depleted in the coastal belt. There is nothing left to minimise the intensity of the next cyclone or flash flood. The ecological rape in the coastal belt should stop forthwith. During May 1998 thousands of people in eastern Orissa died of heat wave. Experts attributed it to the absence of breeze from the bay of Bengal. Ironically this time coastal people could not face the too much and too strong wind from the Bay. As a retaliation, nature has uprooted the all trees across the cyclone stretch and has exposed the state to another bout of heat wave.[10] Past deed has the seed of destruction. The encroachment into the flood zones of rivers, by the refugees, has been occurring ever since the density of population has been rising inexorably. It is this population pressure related encroachment of the flood zones that is the root cause of ever increasing flood related losses in India. Deforestation aggravates the problem but aforestation can not get rid of it.

It was said that the super cyclone, which occurred in 29_{th} October 1999 in Orissa was the greatest horrendous event of the century in the country. It has tormentingly affected the advance regions of Orissa. But the recent earthquake which occurred on 26th Jan 2001 in Gujrat is most horrible unprecedented event of India's history. The situation has become more grim and grave than any natural calamity of the past. The devastation both physical and psychological is enormous. The shock among the people of Kuch and Ahmedabad has overtaken all emotions. In some houses after the quake none was left to shed tears. Entire atmosphere after the event has become cool and calm. The scene of devastation and cries of victims is not easily one believable, unless one sees in own eye. No description will be adequate to depict the real story.

Death toll continuously increases after the calamity. Volunteers and rescue operators are disposing the dead bodies and carcasses. Stench emanating from bloated bodies, decomposed beyond recognition and animal carcasses makes the situation worse. Inflow of patients in the hospitals are ever increasing. Earth movers and dumpers are used to remove the dead bodies of man and animal together. Missionaries, NGOs and State administration are making preparation for mass burial. Lack of desanitisation measures and water purification may cause severe health hazards in the towns. Plight of poor people and patients in the hospital seems to be getting worse by each passing day. Being hopeless some patients are leaving the hospital and going back by keeping faith on God. It is very difficult for the people to overcome the psychological trauma.

10.4. ECONOMIC EFFECTS

The earthquake like the super cyclone of Orissa has wreaked a greater havoc on the state economy. Many economic activities where majority of the population ekes out their living have been raped and ruined by this earthquake. It may take more than a decade to achieve the status quo. All most all social overheads and infrastructures are destroyed. Schools, hospitals, dispensaries, colleges, libraries, clubs, go-downs, post offices, banks, cooperatives etc are partially or totally destroyed. All these listing of damages is an indicative of the economic cost (or loss) of recent event. This also depicts the picture of reconstruction works warranted in the region. We need to look afresh. A comprehensive plan for restoration and rebuilding the state's economy needs to be chalked out urgently.

The problem of earthquake, cyclone or flood is multi dimensional in nature, which varies spatially and temporally. These problems constitute a set of structural factors to economic development of the state. Economic effects of any calamity differ among regions. More developed and economically diversified regions can recover more quickly. Their coping capacity is better. The poor regions are most severely affected. The regions more vulnerable to weather and climate are the worst sufferers of flood or cyclone. Economic effects of any natural calamity can be classified as direct and indirect. **The direct effects** are tangible and monetarily quantified by various agencies. It includes: (a) loss of capital, destruction of houses, roads, bridges, go-downs, factories, irrigation facilities and (b) loss of stocks of consumables, disruption of production activities, reduction of income, loss of jobs, business, livestock, fishing, crop loss etc . **Indirect effects** include loss of lifetime saving and assets and potential earning, disruption of employment sources, artificial shortages, inflationary situations, spread of antisocial elements, donation to relief fund etc. Black marketeers, hoarders capitalise out of panic situations[11] Balance of payments worsens because of the decline and disruption of exports. Public authorities are confronted with a heavy rise in social expenditures on medicine, relief, subsidies, housing and investment for the purpose of reconstructing the community assets destroyed in the natural disasters

In the **short run** the disaster causes loss of human life, animals and distorts the ecological balances. It injures kills and destroys. It causes emotional stress and trauma. It ransacks home and business, and causes economic hardships and spells financial ruin for many. And the people hit worst are the poor, women and children. The threat of an epidemic looms large as survivors are spending their days in the midst of carcasses, In the **longrun** it leaves an unbearable scar and gives a set back to the natural growth and development process of the region. It further entrenches and exacerbates poverty and unemployment and interrupts and sometimes reverses the economic progress of the backward regions of the state in achieving a self-reliant development. In the face of tardy and sluggish growth of the economy all disasters like flood, earthquake and cyclone or drought distorts the smooth functioning of the economy and puts an extraneous and very weighty impediment on the development process. It nullifies the progress achieved and creates very strong obstacle for planned developmental efforts of the region. Economic theory offers no satisfactory solution to this intractable problem. Economists here offer mere sops in the form of financial compensation to the disaster-hit people. But Govt's project for rehabilitating the victims may head towards spectacular failure if it has no clear-cut vision

10.5. POLITICS OF RELIEF

There is always the pressure on the Centre to declare it a "national calamity of rarest severity", which is the stipulation of 10th Finance Commission.[5] Declaration is essential to get international funding for reconstruction for the ravaged districts. Centre can impress the World Bank for soft loan if devastation is declared as the national calamity. According to the provisions made by Finance Commission the affected state has to submit a memorandum with detail calculations of cost of relief and rehabilitation. This is to be vetted by a committee consisting of the deputy Chairman of the Planning commission and others.

Political rivalry in the state is threatening to muddy the massive effort. Politicians get the scope to garner popularity in the state. The different political parties are accusing each other and politicising the issue of Earthquake. But biggest natural disaster in living memory of the century too becomes an occasion for the leaders to play miserable politics. Dissident group is critical to show how their present leader is inefficient and not caring enough. Other leaders of other party are busy in gaining cheap popularity and very eager to appear in TV or appear in front page of any newspaper. Due to these pressures the Government tries to depict a conservative estimate of the damages and deaths. The bureaucracy has the inherent tendency to underestimate the loss and tolls. As if the earthquake has been created by the present Govt. Party infighting is an impeding factors in the handling the catastrophe of such gigantic proportion. A responsible Government and a sensible opposition are expected not only to stir themselves beyond politics to cope and manage with this national disaster like this but also are expected to learn big lessons for the future adaptability and preparedness. Every minister and central authorities usually assure that there is "no dearth of funds" for undertaking relief measures. Relief materials pour everyday from different parts and different sources of the country and abroad. People do not repair the repairables in the hope of getting some relief aid from the public authority. Some try to exploit the situation to their personal benefit. Now some get the nice opportunity of stylising themselves as the patriotic leaders of the locality. There are some groups who sometimes guide and misguide the outside relief teams. Govt. should tighten the law and order situation during this abnormal period to ensure security to the survivors and the relief workers.

Announcements of made by state administration are hasty palliatives. Their promises depict confusion between relief and reconstruction. One is urgent, the other required careful thinking. Relief attends to immediate sufferings. It involves quicker rescue and emergency medical aid. Speed is vital as this action saves life and property. But Reconstruction and rehabilitation are concerned with the future quality of the rest of the survivors life and of their children/grand children thereafter. Speed may be useful but it is not the most important goal. What matters more is life long satisfaction, an accurate assessment of and response to the victim's own desires and needs.

10.6. EFFECTIVE DISASTER MANAGEMENT:

Disaster management is very much crucial not only to meet the immediate requirement but also to reduce its long-term adverse implications on the development process. The coping capacity to these calamitous situations in India is very weak. Backward regions are badly equipped to deal with such events. They have a poor and less flexible administrative system, a lower potential to benefit from previous learning and experience and have inadequate technological infrastructure. Relief and reconstruction strategy of the disaster-affected area must focus on:

(i) restoration of physical damages

(ii) promotion of socio economic development and

(iii) prevention and amelioration of future disaster events.

But the major shortcoming of these programmes are that they are isolated and most discrete and are not part of any comprehensive integrated development plan. Any plan for integrated development of Disaster prone areas (IDDPA) must be based upon the following key factors:

(a) Organisational set up for disaster management

(b) Strong Infrastructural base for IDDPA

(c) Strategy of relief, rehabilitation and reconstruction (SRRR) and

(d) National Policy for IDDPA

Man's response has been focused primarily on relief activity. And Indian meteorological department has only developed a scientific INSAT based cyclone warning system. There is no scientific forecasting about earthquake. As a result the actual and potential consequences of each disaster event are becoming more serious and increasingly global in scale. Disaster management means planned and systematic approach for solving problems in the wake of disasters. An analysis of the present strategy of development of disaster prone areas reveals that it is all based on ad hoc approaches. Even now Indian planners have not recognised disasters as a crucial factor in planning for development. Hence there is the need for the development of these areas on the basis of an integrated approach with a definite regional policy for these areas. Presently it has extended to mainly to relief operations and reconstruction during the post-calamity period. All Relief operations are only palliatives. It does not solve the perennial problem. But role of the public authority should extend from pre-disaster preparedness to rescue, relief and long term reconstruction and development of the affected area. Important areas of disaster management should be: prevention, preparedness, warning, evaluation, rescue, correct identification, relief operation, rehabilitation, reconstruction, assessment and financial arrangements.

The incidence of all natural calamities varies across regions and time .No standard prescription for redressal of the problem will be appropriate for specific region. The present strategy of development of DPAs reveals that they are all uncoordinated and adhoc addendum. Even now planners in India have not recognised disasters as a crucial factor in planning for the development Hence there is need for a new multi pronged approach to mitigate the severity of post –disaster conditions of the people. The new approach should be an integrated one with definite regional policy for the sustained development of these disaster prone areas(DPAs).The strategy of development of DPAs is not the concern of any single ministry or any Govt. department such as Finance, Revenue Agriculture, irrigation, health, education, rural electrification, animal husbandry, forestry, roads, building, cooperation, and planning. Therefore an integrated development of DPAs has the real danger of floundering on the rock of departmentalism. Hence to overcome these problems it is imperative to devise an organisational and managerial innovations with in a sound functional framework. What we need is a permanent and functional disaster management organisation, not a knee-jerk action Committee with some ministers with dogmatic ideas and some bureaucrats, with their rigid mindset. They must be scientifically equipped to foresee disaster possibilities and move with specially trained rapid action forces (TRAF). Such an agency will be certainly handle the crises better than the present semi-existent agencies/departments. Intense sufferings today should become the cornerstone for future policy.

10.7. NEED FOR NIDM

In every country there are many research Institutes on disaster management. To cite few examples: Disaster Research Center of Ohio University, Natural Hazard Research, University of Chicago, Natural Hazard Research and Application Information Center of Colorado, World Meteorological organisation, Geneva, UN disaster Relief Office (UNDRO) Geneva, International Disaster Institute, London, Disaster Research Unit, Bradford University, Disaster research Center, University of Delware are doing wonderful research work which significantly contributes to the society. In India the public authority suffer from inadequate and improper understanding about different types of disasters and their consequences and remedies, be it Kalahandi's drought related hunger, Orissa's super cyclone or super flood, Latuer's quake or Bhopals gas tragedy. We have only instant and hasty understanding. We respond very erratically and randomly to the post disaster crisis. Therefore a research team has to be encouraged to disseminate information and generate proper understanding about the problem6. There should be one independent National Research Institute of Disaster Management in India

10.8. MARKET FAILURE

Under the present policy of globalisation and free market regime, state has a vital role to play. Laws and regulations are to be enacted and enforced to protect the survivors. Market forces can not deliver goods to the people in DPAs. Sustainable livelihood, reconstruction and rehabilitation works and permanent infrastructural overheads can not be provided by the private sector. Worldwide Globalisation movement has little solution to this kind of disaster-related problems. Trickle down theory of the development planning can not be relied upon either.

So effective people's participation is warranted in the reconstruction works. The speedy completion of relief phase is crucial to the success of the reconstruction programmes as the community start to take over the responsibility for their own future. An extended relief phase as in Uttarkashi and many other places would severely cripple the ability of the communities to take decisions and resume normal life. They may be caught in a 'dependency syndrome'. In the process of reconstruction the affected people should make their own choices. Benefactors should seize this opportunity to improve their thinking and life style. But there should be community participation. The special needs of the victims should be carefully understood. External solutions should not be considered always superior. Western solutions should not be thrust upon the affected communities. The reconstruction drive should not be designed to force the recipient to switch to the benefactor's value system. Otherwise, the danger is that despite all good intentions, the rehabilitation project will falter not only physically but also leave the people there less confident, frustrated, and unhappier than ever before. These are very crucial factors that the NGOs, donor agencies and state administration should consider. Otherwise it would be a fait accompli.

REFERENCES

Awasthi A & Ranga Rao SP(1982),*Crisis Administration in India*, Sterling Pub.,Delhi

Cuny, F C ,(1983) *Disasters and Development*, Oxford University Press

Dhawan, B D(1993),Coping with Flood in Himalayan Rivers, *Economic & Political weekly*,Vol.28(18),May, PP 849-852

IFRC(1998) *World Disasters Report*, International Federation of Red Cross, Oxford Univ press

Jain, NK (1982) Disaster preparedness in India, Joint Assistance Centre, New Delhi.

Mohanty, Bidyut (1993) Orissa Famine of 1866,: demographic and economic consequences, *Economic and Political Weekly*,Vo.28(1-2) Jan,pp55-66

Oliver, J(1981) Disaster management in developing Countries: some contrasts, *Disaster Management*,Vol.1(4),Oct-Dec, PP.155-62

Patel, BP(1994) Marthawada Earthquake, *Economic and Political Weekly*,Vol.29(8),Feb,Pp401-405

Raghavulu, CV (1982) Disaster Preparedness: a study in Community Perspective, ARTIC, Hyderabad.

11

Sustainable Tourism Under Globalisation Regime

All sectors of Indian Economy seem to be vibrating after globalisation. It has generated an atmosphere of over optimism of instant economic growth. There is hyper growth of the tertiary sector, in which tourism constitutes the major component. The entire tertiary sector is becoming highly elitist, information intensive and sophisticated. Its labour absorption capacity has remained very low. And the tourism sector under free marketism is likely to cause more environmental loading and degradation. Private agents in their scrambling for profit may despoil the very carrying capacity of tourism. Therefore this chapter makes out a case for having a sustainable and indigenous process of green tourism, which warrants a sound tourism infrastructure through a proactive public policy.

Tourism is the second largest industry of the world and sixth largest industry in India. Tourism comprises the largest component of the tertiary sector[44]. It constitutes the major item in the world trade, which is growing at a faster rate than the world trade in tangible goods. It has now become a highly organised industry representing about 12 percent of world's gross income. World's revenue from this business has been constantly growing at a faster rate .In developing countries Tourism is also one of the largest industries with fastest expansion in its range and dimension. It is an industry with great employment potential. In fact one in every 16 workers worldwide owns his or her job to tourism sector. It has emerged as the most lucrative business of the world, having tremendous potentiality for earning foreign exchange, yielding tax revenue to the state, promoting ancillary industries, generating income and employment and developing backward regions through various linkage effects[45].

11.1. TOURISM POTENTIAL OF INDIA

Tourism as a sector of economic significance received the widest recognition after II world war it is considered as smokeless hospitality industry and leisure or entertainment industry. In India it was duly emphasised during its planning era. But it is given a fresh lease of life under the globalisation regime. India has immense tourism resource potential. Indian Tourism involves a wide range of economic activities and services. It is the most profitable business for the agents and actors. The most obvious ones are: (I) accommodation and hospitality and (ii) travel and transportation. There are however many other ancillary services and informal activities having direct effects and bearing on tourism. There is also high potential for self employment in this sector. It provides a vast spectrum of employment[46] starting from highly trained mangers of 5 star hotels to sales girls, room boys, handicraft artisans, to transport workers. Ancillary services having direct connectivity with tourism are: handicrafts, souvenir industry, horticulture, floriculture, leisure and entertainment services, and activities of all personnel dealing with tourists across the counter in customs, immigration, airports, airlines, railway stations, ferry services, museums, bus terminals, taxi stands, banks, medicals, police stations, post offices, communication, advertising, shopping centres, sports and many other organisations both in the private and public sector.

India has the most unique historic and cultural mosaic. Its civilization is the unique combination of Vedic, Islamic and western streams. It has very rich tradition, monuments, temples, sculptures and paintings. Its geographical features are both colourful and varied. It has the best beaches of the world, with irresistible combination of sea, sun and sands. It has chain of bird's sanctuaries, crocodile sanctuaries, lakes, springs, waterfalls, national parks, wealth of wild life .It has variety of religions and languages. It has number of fairs and festivals. 'Product India' boasts of being copious, exceptional and unique in many ways. It provides real psychological gratification to the tourists.

11.2. IMPACT OF GLOBALISATION

Unfortunately it faces a great contradiction now. There is now euphoria of 'high- tech-efficiency' around the globe. The influence of globalisation movement, fait accompli, has now become all pervasive. There is now over optimism and over enthusiasm of instant change and sudden economic growth. There is hyper growth of the tertiary sector of India. There is excessive growth of many superfluous things and activities like financial services, entertainment etc. Its growth acceleration is attributable to half-real and half-illusory output. With growth of entertainment services during the last decade, Indian Economy seems to follow the dictum of Cicero i.e. "If people can not be fed with food, feed them on circus". It is nothing but tittytainment, which is strongly endorsed by the present globalisation model. The service sector predominance is premature replication of a feature of the industrially advanced countries. Thus we notice a clear trend of growth of economy without involving the majority of our people or reflecting their needs and requirements. This type of growth is jobless, ruthless, rootless and voiceless .It may be noted here that these elitist services have relatively low labour absorption.[47] This development process is biased against the wage goods. There is appropriation of the surplus by the class of non-producers, consultants and brokers. The path of tourism development in India has become more imitative than any other sector. It is the impact of transnational tourism culture. It is a dangerous trend for our economy and society. Tourism sector, like any other industry is also tending to be more capital intensive and information intensive[48]. The external advocacy on the virtues of globalisation is found convenient vehicle by the urban-rich-elite class for promoting their vested self-interests. It provides enough scope to follow the model of 'cronyism' for the ruling party and bureaucracy. Structural Adjustment programme inevitably leads to 'crony capitalism'[49]. True but insidious western cultural influences are inherent in western FDI, technology, foreign travel, food, dress, language, freedom of media, internet etc .The negative consequences of Economic Reforms now travel far and wide not only for specific industries, groups or regions but for the whole economy, polity and people at large. It is never friendly to the poor, the vulnerable section, backward regions nor to the natural environment. Its success can at best be treated as a "pyrrhic victory", when 'means win and ends lose'.

11.3. ENIRONMENTAL IMPLICATIONS

The greatest irony is that under the regime of globalisation and free marketism, the developers and agents operating in the tourism sector are in their height of avarice and greed. In the process for scrambling for profit they have inherent tendency to become insensitive to every thing, more so to the environment. There is a very close relationship between tourism development and the impact of tourism on natural environment. After global economic integration there is now blind imitation of the transnational tourism culture. More severe competition is likely to be among the developers in the private sector agents to over exploit the tourism sector and consequently the natural environment. Globalisation endorses the policy of 'industrial Darwinism'. The order of the day is survival of the fittest. That survival instinct obviously tends to cause more extraction, more emission and more energy consumption in the tourism business. In the Indian tourism sector, there will be over use of environmental resources like over boating, over hunting, over pumping, over fishing, over cutting, over trekking, over motoring, poached wild life, noise pollution, water pollution, more air conditioning, more sewage dumping, etc. Tourism development in India at micro level is very small, profitable but short sighted. Private agent continues to use it as the 'Common Property Resources'[50] till he gets profit. He never thinks about the future viability of his own business. The successful youth today never thinks about his grand children. But the cumulative impact of tourism activities at the macro level poses a major environmental challenge. Facing this challenge is very costly. It involves substantial costs and shifts. But not facing the challenge is more costly and disastrous for the entire tourism sector.

With western imitation through free market policy, rapidity in tourism sector may result in creation of new tourism facilities. These developments in many cases lead to competition and conflict .In turn they have generated a wide range of deleterious environmental impacts. It has many negative social and cultural impacts. The local people of the tourist centres stand to lose in the current process of tourism development. It has become another element of the destructive process, which exploits the local population, damages the environment, promotes consumerism, widens the gap between rich and poor and reinforces the global status quo. India is turning into giant theme parks for the entertainment of the affluent class of the planet. The global structure is resulting in the lethal dependence of third world countries and exploitation and destruction of natural environment.

11.4. GREEN TOURISM

Hence India needs to adopt a new set of values. In order to have a distinguished niche in the international tourism market India has to develop its tourism in its own way and vision. Dreaming is rather more relevant but imitation most disastrous. Planning is very much necessary. Therefore the role of the state is very much indispensable. It is wrong to reduce the role of the public sector in tourism. At least in the present period of ideological vacuum of statelessness at least we must appreciate the positive role of the planning, in building the infrastructural base of tourism. Stronger infrastructure is conducive for healthy tourism. Without the umpiring of the state the private sector will bring such kind of tourism which may be attractive but deceptive. We are pursuing the efficient and profitable path of tourism development. High efficiency now implies high profitability which, willy nilly it results in high environmental intervention. Healthy tourism may result in unhealthy environment. Unmanaged tourism can be disastrous but organised tourism can only contribute to the genuine prosperity of the region. Suitable policy of the state can ensure 'green tourism', which can flourish only in an eco friendly atmosphere. Sustainable tourism can reconcile the imperatives of both tourism and environment .In this pursuit of 'green tourism' more resources are necessary to reinforce the ecosystem rather than making it vulnerable to risks from unplanned activities or neglect.

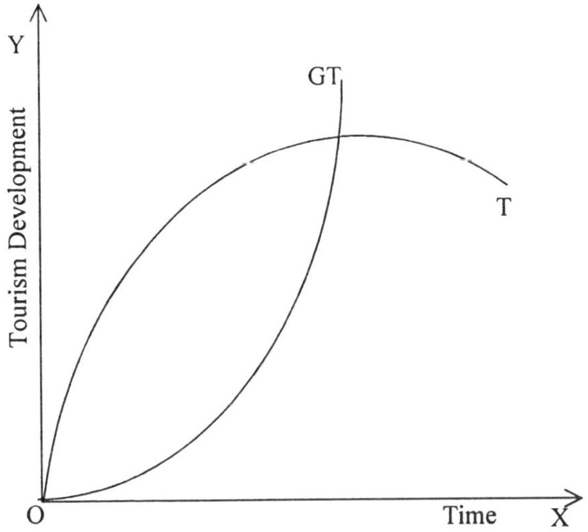

Fig. 11.1: Sustainable Tourism Vs Efficient Tourism

The Fig. 11.1 explains the difference between efficient tourism and sustainable tourism. The Efficient path (E) of tourism development is very impressive but non sustainable It curls down in the long run. It undermines its own base(carrying capacity) in the long run.. But S path is sustainable though very unimpressive in the beginning. Sustainability implies efficiency but not vice versa. The sustainable path has no maximum point. It is slow but steady. Sustainability implies economic efficiency but not vice versa. The sustainability can not be ensured only by the standard cost- benefit formula. It should be revised so as to include the environmental cost of any tourism project.

Thus :

Green Tourism = Tourism development + Value of Environmental Services/ Resources – Cost of Environmental damage .

Therefore the standard cost benefit formula should be revised as:

$\Sigma(B_t - C_t - E_t)(1+r)^{-t} > 0$

and $s > d_k + d_n$

Where: B_t = Benefits from tourism

s = Savings of the Tourism sector

C_t = Cost of tourism

d_n = Depreciation of natural capital

E_t = Environmental damages

d_k = Depreciation of man-made capital

Concern for environment should not be dismissed as obsession environmental romantics. Environmentalism is not anti tourism, it is not an irritant but a demand on tourism. Tourists, themselves have now become more conscious of environmental virtues. Environmental attributes attract more tourists because of its outstanding scenic beauty and recreational values. But the paradox of present trend of Indian tourism is that in the long run it tends to impair and even destroy the very qualities of the environment, which attracts people.

11.5. PERILOUS GROWTH

Hyper tourism development emerging from western route places undue pressure on the regenerative or assimilation capacity of the environment. It leads to congestion, erosion of quality and physical deterioration of various tourism facilities. Over crowding despoils its own 'carrying capacity' and brings in its wake certain environmental hazards[51]. Many elements inherent in the present trend of tourism development under the liberalised regime run contrary to the notion of sustainability. Green tourism can not subsist upon a deteriorating environmental condition. Therefore the future prospects is one of retrogression or at best stagnation. It is now difficult to dream of having a sustainable tourism, which may be slow, unimpressive but steady and meaningful to the rural people.

Thus higher growth of tourism sector is perilous to itself. Because its basic raw materials are:

1. Landscape,scenic beauty
2. Water bodies,streams,sea,lakes and lagoons
3. Invigoating climate
4. Forests and vegetation
5. Exotic flora and rich fauna
6. Wealth of Wildlife
7. Ethnographic museums
8. Religious melting pots

All these resources are part of the natural heritage of mankind. India is a vast repository with all these varied environmental attractions. These are susceptible to over exploitation in the wake of tourism development. There is imminent fatigue in the tourism activities. It destroys its own base upon which it grows. Therefore present pattern of 'cul de sac tourism' has a built-in doom. It has to ultimately die its natural death, unless reorientation is done.

Therefore tourism sector or any of its problems should not be viewed in isolation. It must be contexualised in the broader liberalised framework. Pattern of tourism should not only be tourist oriented but also be region specific and people based. The guiding principle of 'green tourism' is environmental sustainability, which underscores that industry can not afford to overlook the growing gravity of environmental issues connected with the tourist destinations. Without this principle we are in the process of killing the "tourism goose which is laying golden eggs" of high profit and high psychological gratification to the tourists.

Green tourism emphasises conservation but not consumption, protection not production, future not present, quality not quantity. At theoretical level a strong agreement has emerged to reconcile the conflict between tourism development and environmental preservation. But in practice there is the persistence of a very large gap between the two[5252] Das Kumar, Developmentalism, Environmentalism and Decentralism, Utkal Economic Papers, Vol,IX 1997. Green tourism can not subsist upon a deteriorating environmental condition. Therefore the future indicators of sustainable tourism can be identified. Sustainable tourism may be slow ,unimpressive but steady and meaningful to the rural people.

However there are several inhibiting factors, which constrain the growth of eco-tourism in third world countries. It is very difficult to reconcile and make them compatible. The real challenge lies in implementation. The question is how to translate this notion into reality. It can be illustrated in the following tourism model(Fig 11.2) pertaining to any individual tourism project. This model shows that both developmental objectives and environmental objectives are reconciled in the policy and planning. After implementation there is need for evaluation and making process reforms and project redesigning. The environmental impact assessment is essential component at the time of implementation.

According to Groupe Development (2000) of France the checklist comprises 16 indicators to evaluate the sustainability of tourist sites. These are:

1. Indicators of Physical impact
2. Indicators of Safety measures
3. Indicators of Health facilities
4. Indicators of Cultural properties
5. Indicator of liquid waste disposal
6. Indicators of solid waste disposal
7. Indicators of Water consumption

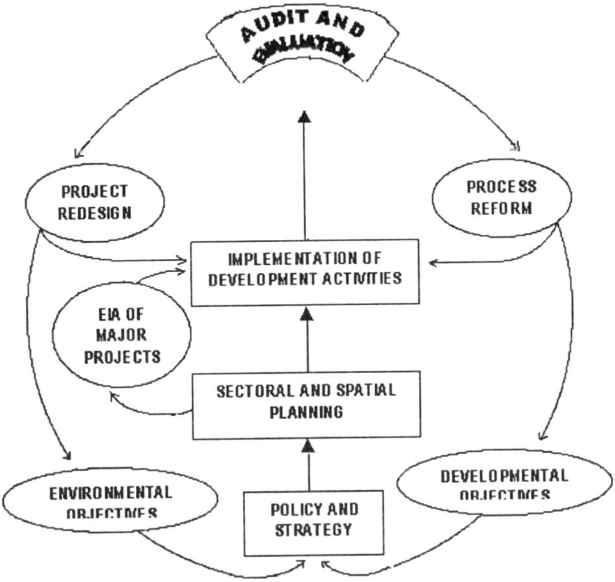

Fig. 11.2. Sustainability of Tourism Project

8. Indicators of the impact on
9. Indicators of local involvement
10. Indicators of the adoption of new technology
11. Indicators of child protection
12. Indicators of the existence of labour protection
13. Indicators of continuing training for staff
14. Indicators of Visual aspect
15. Indicators of Job creation
16. Indicators of control over development process local production/consumption

This check list comprises 16 ratios corresponding to the above cited 16 indicators. The use of this check list is based on a comparison between the reference ratios and actual ratios for each tourist sites. Then all tourist sites should be classified for appropriate spatial planning.

11.6. RURAL TOURISM

Rural tourism is always sustainable, Both short term and long term planning, implementing and monitoring are vital in avoiding damages to the rural areas. Environmental management, local involvement and realistic planning are all crucial if rural tourism is to be sustainable and make a positive contribution to improvement of living standard of the village people . Rural tourism as a segment of the tourism industry, should be more important in India, which is a country with spectacular natural attractions, seasides, high mountains, rainforests or herds of exotic animals. However its attractive natural and cultural landscapes with small villages, combined with traditional hospitality are able to offer pleasant experiences to the kind of tourists who are looking for relaxation and recreation in a calm setting.

Rural tourism development can play important role in diversification of the tourism supply and in the creation of more complex and colourful country image. On the other hand rural tourism is not the end but a means to stimulate economic growth, to increase the living standard of the rural people. It should be an integral part of rural development process. Rural tourism should include a range of activities ,services and amenities provided by the people of the countryside, farmers and fisherman, milkman, weavers etc to attract tourists to their locality in order to generate extra income from their occupations. Rural tourism has the potential to be the most effective strategy of regional economic development. It is a very complex notion being determined by economic, ecological and socio cultural factors. The following indicators might act as useful measures of those factors that together contribute to the sustainable rural tourism development in India.

Indicators of Rural Tourism

Indicators	*Measures and Features*
Economic diversity	% Share of different economic activities in the total tax incomes
Employment generation	Number of jobs created in tourism sector(full time equivalent)% of local employees to all workers
Contribution to the locality	% of tax income generated by tourism only
Planning Process	Existences of local/regional plan for development
Tourism planning	Existence of tourism development plan
Peoples involvement	% of number of locally owned tourist business to total number of tourist operators
Local control	Existence of formal measures (public hearing) to ensure local control over development planning and implementation
Energy consumption	%of renewable energy sources to non renewable energy sources
Waste Management	% of waste receiving treatment % of household with proper sewage system
Education &Training	Distribution of tourism employees by educational level% of tourism employee participating in on the job training % of local people involved in tourism with training and education
Social Stress	Number of tourists in the locality per annum Ratio of tourist to local population per annum
Attractiveness	List of natural and cultural resources
Area protection	% protected area compared to the whole territory of the destination
Local satisfaction	Peoples' perception of tourism impacts in the local community
Tourist satisfaction	Overall satisfaction of tourists in terms of quality and price% of the repeat visits

11.7. CONCLUDING NOTE

It is a great challenge for us and for the policy makers. Both the 'need to develop' and 'need to protect' are necessary. Tourism being the multi dimensional activity should not flounder in the rock bottom of departmentalism. An holistic view should be taken keeping all the aspects of tourism and ensuring complete coordination between different departments of the Govt. such as Commerce, Finance, Civil Aviation, Urban and Land development, Home and External Affairs.Integrated policy is necessary which can encompass various aspects like property rights, carrying capacity area specific environmental impact assessment and monitoring in order to strike a balance. Fragmented nature of decision making in the past for protecting the environment has failed in many respects in regulating environmental resources. Emphasis should be given to creating necessary tourism infrastructure along the connecting routes to different tourist destinations. Therefore the present trend of tourism development needs to be reoriented into an activity that promotes cooperation rather than competition, directs people to appreciate quality of life rather than excessive consumption and maintains a clean environment.

The particular need is to establish more integrated approach to tourism development planning and environmental management. Such process should be comprehensive in scope, coordinative in function and collaborative in style. The pattern of production and consumption in the tourism sector, which would be environment friendly necessarily, calls for govt. intervention, regulation and perspective planning. It can never emerge from free play of market forces. Market can not solve the very problem that it creates. Healthy environment and healthy tourism do not coexist automatically. Invisible hand does not work. So State intervention is inescapable. Therefore we need to invigorate and revitalise the public sector and promote its efficiency. We need radical resurrection but not whole sale retreat of the public sector. Strong public sector is the prerequisite for optimising the efficiency of private sector business in any sector including the tourism sector. Both public and private sector should mutually interact and appreciate each other's role in achieving sustainability in tourism sector. Therefore we need to redefine the role of the state. We need to have proactive public policy for tourism. We need to develop sound infrastructural base, which is conducive for sustainable tourism .We need to devise appropriate monetary and fiscal policy to develop 'green tourism' instead of profit driven western tourism. We need to:

- redistribute the tourist flows
- diversify the tourism activities
- coordinate among tourism agents
- have proper Indian vision and plan
- make harmonious development
- have focussed high quality professionalism
- convert environmental features into facilities
- ensure safety and security to the tourists

Thus an integrated policy with holistic approach is necessary which can encompass various aspects like property rights, carrying capacity, and area-specific environmental impact assessment. and monitoring in order to strike a balance between :

a) Economic feasibility

b) Social desirability and

c) Environmental sustainability.

REFERENCES

Bhatia A K (!982) Tourism Development: principles and practices, Sterling Pub.,Delhi

Das Kumar(1994), Profile of Global Tourism in India, Indian Journal of Marketing, Vol.XXI (11)

Puri RK (1990) Tourism and Human Resource Development, Employment News,April 13-20

Seth R(1996) Tourism in India: an overview,Yojana,Vol40(8)

Tisdell C (1995) Investing in Eco Tourism:assessing its Economics, Tourism Economics,Vol.1(4)

12
Sustainable Rural Development

Central planning after independence resulted in inefficiencies and delays in carrying out centrally conceived schemes and plans for achieving rural development. This chapter provides the theoretical synthesis between multi objective and multi level Planning in a decentralized framework. The decentralised system of rural economic development can ensure: (i) spatial balance, (ii) sectoral balance and (iii) operational balance. It argues that the genuine people's participation can promote social synergy, which ensures sustainable prosperity for the people.

Central Planning and Administration were considered necessary to guide and control the economy and to integrate and unity nations that were emerging from long periods of colonial rule. It was believed that Central Planning Industrial investments concentrated in one or two major metropolitan centres would 'tickle down' and spread throughout the economy to alleviate poverty and generate income and employment at the sub-national levels. The capital mobilised through savings would be reinvested, thereby expanding production and employment, raising income, drawing large number of people into productive process and eventually pushing the poor into a stage of self-sustaining economic growth. Regional disparity would gradually be lessened and the majority of people would benefit from the continued growth and development.

But, by the end of 1960's it was widely recognised that central planning had not achieved these goals in all developing countries of the world. The economic growth remained sluggish even where the growth rates were high, only a small group usually benefited from the increased national production. Income disparities between rich and poor and among regions widened. The living standard of the poorest section has declined and the number of people living in absolute poverty, in the rural sector has increased (World Bank, 1975). Many development planners and administrators began questioning the effectiveness of strategies based primarily on central planning framework aiming at increased industrial output and challenged the existing theories of economic development. At present the governments in developing countries are decentralising development planning and management responsibilities not only because political groups seeking new roles for regions and units of administrations continue to bring pressure on them, but because they have discovered that the over-concentration of decision-making and management responsibilities at the centre leads to inefficiencies and delays in carrying out centrally conceived schemes and plans for achieving rural development.

The traditional model of central planning was based on the assumption of a single central decision-making unit aiming at achieving a uni-dimensional goal such as maximization of social welfare, GNP, rate of economic growth or minimization of inequality, poverty or unemployment. The policy analyses are developed on the assumption of a wonderland having no other decision-making unit, while external 'spillover effects' are frequently excluded. Recently however, there is a growing concern of the existence and relevance of spillover effects between both economic agents and decision-making units (region or state). A simultaneous analysis of all the relevant policy objectives and of all, the relevant decision units complicates and makes the traditional policy and programming models inappropriate to a considerable degree.

This chapter aims at providing a theoretical synthesis between multi-objective and multi-level planning in a decentralised framework. It gives a brief introduction to multi-objective programming and multi-level planning and highlights the coordination problems. Integrated planning strategies for a system divided into a set of sub-systems require methods of resolution of goal conflict or interest conflict emerging from the interaction among the components of the system. Hence, a decentralised system of decision-making should guarantee allocation of resources which must ensure a meaningful compromise among the various policies of the different spatial segments.

The information and data on the following three aspects, *inter alia*, are essential in order to analyse the interaction among the spatial components of the decentralised system and the complexity involved in the decentralised policy or decision-making levels.

(i) **Linkage pattern** : It refers to the nature and magnitude of interaction and interdependence subsisting among the various components of the system.

(ii) **Interior-conflict** : It refers to the conflict that exists among the various priorities and goals of each component. It may be termed as intra-component (intra-regional) conflict.

(iii) **Exterior-conflict** : It refers to the conflict that exits among the various interests and strategies that are adopted by several competing decision units. It may be termed as inter-component (inter-regional) conflict.

The linkage pattern and interdependence are better represented and explained by structural models, which describe all interactions within and between the components of the system. For example, an inter-regional input-output model describes the functions economic relationships within and among the regions of a national economy.

Interior conflict is properly resolved by the use of a multi-objective programming in which a vector optimization problem represents the conflict existing among a set of multi-dimensional objectives. For example, a multi-dimensional programming resolves the friction between the maximum production of industrial goods and a maximum of environmental quality within the given spatial component. Hence, a multi-objective programming aims at dealing with multi-dimensional nature of choices and conflictual options of a given region.

Hence, a multi-level planning aims at coordinating either as a top-down centralisation policy or a bottom-up decentralisation policy between different decision levels in order to eliminate the sub-optimal or less efficient social choices. Figure-12.1 depicts an illustrative representation of such a multi-objective and multi-level policy in a decentralized framework.

This reflects the multi-goal and multi-level conflict profile. It also illustrates the interaction among the various spatial components of the relevant policy strategy. The various goal functions are denoted as $g_1\ g_2 — g_r$ (of a given spatial unit). The model clearly represents a double-choice conflict *viz* between intra-component goals and inter-component interests. The goal conflict emerges from the diverging nature of objectives and priorities within a given

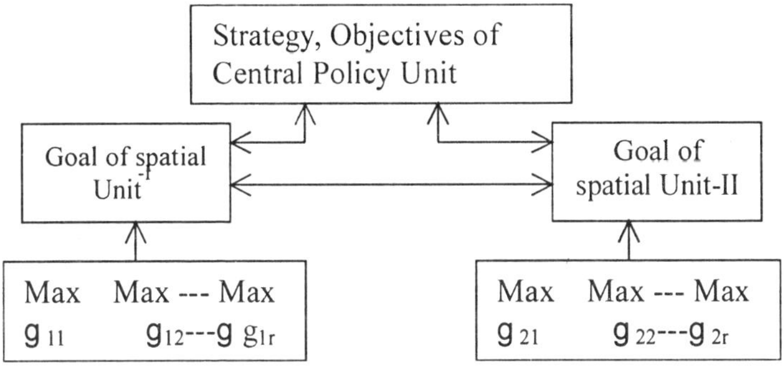

Fig.12.1: Multi-dimensional Decentralised Model

spatial unit in the face of resource constraints. This kind of a problem involving conflictual choice is dealt in the field of multi-objective programming (Bell, et al, 1977). But the conflicts among the spatial units largely emerge from:

(i) Linkage or spillover effects among various spatial components. For example, input-output linkage of a multi-regional system or spatial negative externality etc., are the sources of exterior conflict.

(ii) Competition or rivalry to secure large portion of the scarce resources by the policy units. Spatial components do fight and continuously plead for large percentage of resources which obviously reduces the share of other regions.

Let us conceive of a decentralised system where the policy unit has two regional components. Let they be denoted as x and y. The intra-regional and inter-regional structure of the first region can be represented by means of the following function:

$$A_x = f(a_x, a_y, s_x)$$

Where: a_x denotes a set of relevant variables for region x like volume of employment, sectoral levels of production, emission of pollution, use of fuel and energy consumption level. 'a_y' denotes the vector of the corresponding variables for the second region y. 's_x' represents a vector of all exogenous variables of the first region x.

Analogously one can perceive another function for region y:

$$A_y = f(a_y, a_x, s_y)$$

Where: 'a_y' refers to the set of relevant variables for region y. 'a_x' represents the vector of corresponding variables for region x and s_y is the vector of exogenous variables for region y.

In this multi-regional decentralised system, input-output, linkage, transport flows, migration flows, commuting pattern and environmental externalities are several examples of inter-regional interaction. Such interdependence among the regions (or decentralised unit) can be illustrated by the matrix in figure 12.2.

	Region-x	Region-y
Region x	$a_x\, a_x$	$a_x a_y$
Region y	$a_y\, a_x$	$a_y\, a_y$

Fig. 12.2 : Inter-regional Interaction

In Figure-2, the diagonal cells of the matrix represent intra-regional interaction (including goal-conflicts) while off-diagonal cells represent inter-regional interdependence (including interest-conflict).

However, in this kind of a situation, the structural relationships and interactions are normally constrained by a set of conditions, which identify the action space of the decision units. These constraints may be technological, economic, environmental or institutional. So, the feasible zone of a_x may be represented by m_x such that:

$$a_x \in m_x$$

Analogously the feasible zone of a_y may be denoted by m_y such that $a_y \in m_y$ with the existence of such a constrained situation one can specify the following type of multi-regional and multi-objective programming in a decentralized framework:

For Region – x		*For Region - y*	
Max	*Max——Max*	*Max*	*Max——Max*
g_{x1}	g_{x2} —— g_{xj}	g_{y1}	g_{y1} —— g_{yj}
(a_x)	(a_x) (a_x)	(a_y)	(a_y) (a_y)

For total system

Max *Max——Max*

g_{n1} G_{n2} —— g_{nj}

$(a_x a_y)$ $(a_x a_y)$ $(a_x a_y)$

Subject to

$$a_x \in m_x$$

$$a_y \in m_y$$

and $(a_x a_y) \in m_n$

where $m_x ,\subset M_n$

$m_y ,\subset M_n$ or

$$M_x \cup M_y = M_n$$

By synthesising the regional sub-systems and the total system as a whole, a multi-objective matrix can be obtained.

	Region x	Region y	Total system
Objective g_1 functions			
g_2			
g_j			

Fig. 12.3 : Integrated Policy Framework

In Figure 3, each column represents intra-regional profile of all, the relevant objectives, whereas each row represents the inter-regional profile of given objective function. Thus, the horizontal optimisation yields the maximum value of corresponding objective functions, while the vertical optimisation yields a maximum value of all objective functions within one region. Obviously, both directions involve serious policy contradictions between components and objectives.Therefore, an appropriate compromise framework has to be devised which leads to satisfactory results.

The gaps between the goals of decentralisation and the results of policy implementation in the developing world remain very much wide. In several cases, however, relatively successful decentralisation has taken place, which implies that there do exist factors and conditions in those countries which are conducive to the achievement of the objectives of decentralisation. So, the implementation strategy for decentralisation should attempt to maximise the impact of support factors while at the same time minimise the constraints. It is contended that the reality of the situation in developing countries is such that an incremental implementation strategy clearly articulated and continuously implemented in stages over a long period of time would be politically feasible and would lead to meaningful results.

In many cases, we find that the governments of developing countries enact decentralisation policies that are vague and amorphous in their purposes, goals and scope; leading to confusion among administrators, political leaders and citizens as to what is warranted and how it is to be achieved. Figure 12.4 illustrates the factors that determine the success and failure of decentralisation policies in developing countries.

1. Regional and Local Capacities : An assessment of the regional and local capacities should precede decisions about the scope of decentralisation and the allocation of functions (Gabriel, 1976). Some countries have delegated or developed functions *en masse* without taking into account the fact that state, provincial, district or local organisations in different parts of the country have different

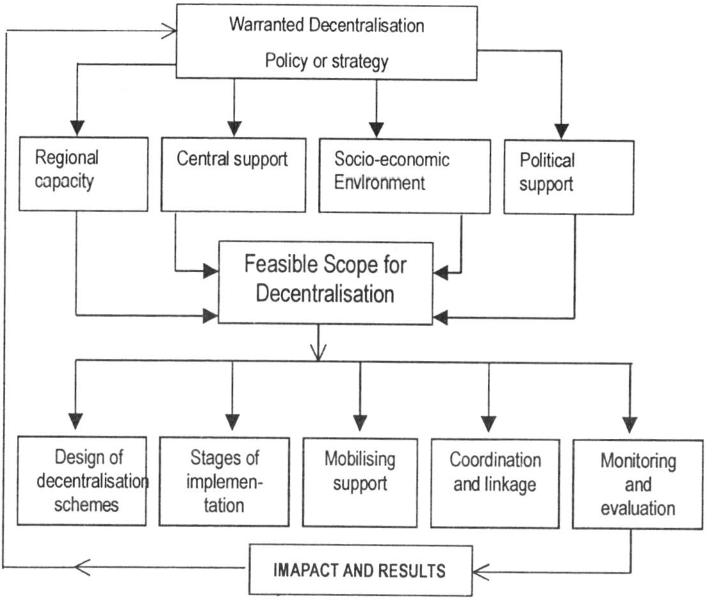

Fig. 12.1 : Feasible Scope for Decentralisation Policies

levels of administrative capacity, different amounts of resources and different levels of commitment to decentralisation.

2. Political Support : Proper attention should be given to determine the extent of political support and opposition to various forms of decentralisation among, the national leaders, high-level administrative officials, field staff, local elites and leaders, before any decision is taken on decentralisation policies and allocation of functions.

3. Central Support : It is very much necessary to gauge the capacity and desire of officials of central administrative agencies to provide financial, technial and managerial support to decentralised organisation to achieve an improvement in the implementation of decentralisation strategies.

4. Environmental Constraints : The existing political set-up, tradition, culture or behavioural characteristics, national economic conditions and trends, the state of development in various regions etc., are very crucial factors in determining the success of decentralisation policies. Although a precise measurement and comprehensive analysis is not possible in most developing countries, proper consideration of potential effects can lead to more carefully designed and executed policies.

After a feasible scope of decentralisation is determined, policies must be translated into programmes and organisational arrangements must be designed for transferring planning and management functions. Secondly, decentralisation can be very successful if the process is incremental and iterative. Those aspects or programmes that are least likely to be opposed and for which there is adequate administrative capacity should be expanded, as the political support and administrative competence increases. Thirdly, the mass media, training and public information programmes and political bargaining must be used widely to forge a base of support for decentralisation policies. Fourthly, means must be found out for reorienting central administrators' perception of their roles from control and direction to support and facilitation. Lastly, the implementation of decentralisation policies must be seen as a continuing process of modifying government structure and procedures as conditions become more conducive to incremental expansions in their scope and application. The ability to adjust and adapt depends on effective monitoring and evaluation process that gauge the pace and impact of decentralisation and from which information can be derived to make policy changes in a more appropriate direction.

Ultimately, decentralisation can be effective only when agencies and actors at the regional and local levels have developed the capacities to perform effectively the planning, decision-making and management functions that are formally granted to them. Their effectiveness as participants in a decentralised system depends on the ability of local organisation to (i) identify development prospects and opportunities, (ii) evolve possible solutions to development problems, (iii) make decisions and resolve conflicts, (iv) mobilise resources and (v) manage development programmes and projects.

Spatial planning in a decentralised framework is the most effective means of illustrating rural 'needs' and priorities. It involves people's participation and, therefore, can promote "social synergy" with internal consistency. The decentralised system of rural economic development will certainly help ensure: (i) spatial balance, (ii) sectoral balance and (iii) operational balance.

By democratic decentralization , priorities, potentials and problems of the rural people can be balanced. It can ensure effective horizontal integration and vertical integration by functional people participation. It can ensure dynamic relation between planning and implementation. It guarantees the effective delivery system by neutralizing the vested interests. Thus all rural development projects should be socially desirable, legally permissible ,technically feasible and environmentally sustainable.

REFERENCE

1. Rural Development Sector Policy Paper, World Bank, Washington DC, 1975, Annex-1-5.
2. See among other works, Bell, et al (1977) – Conflicting objectives in decisions, Wiley, New York and Cochrane JL & M. Zeleny (ed). 1973, Multiple Criteria Decision-making, Univ. of South Carolina Press, Columbia.
3. Gabriel U. (1976), Implementation and Planning for Development – the problem of achieving result, Eastern Regional Organisation for Public Administration, Manila.
4. Das Kumar (1990) Rural Development Through Decentralisation, Discovery Pub House, New Delhi

13
The Epilogue

The pragmatism of globalization of knowledge has generated an over optimism around the globe. It has created an atmosphere of excitement of instant economic growth. It is being projected through out the globe, as an impetus having no alternative. It is being regarded substantively as the growing interdependence and interconnectedness of the world that is the part of the logic of modernity. It is expected to create unprecedented new opportunities for rapid economic development. In fact all sectors of developing countries seems to be vibrating with economic buoyancy. It has generated an atmosphere of excitement of instant economic growth. There is expansion of trade, investment, market, and increase in GNP, productivity, per capita income, profit, efficiency, salary etc. across the globe. Life style of metro people in developing countries has become more attractive , comfortable and fashionable than ever before . But premature replication of features of the industrially advanced countries are observed with developing countries including India. For example the new reforms process of India pursues economic growth to the best of its ability until it is distracted by other social issues like education, health and environment. But in fact this new emerging world economic order poses a great challenge for the developing society. The concern for sustainable development is becoming increasingly louder with the rapidity of economic growth. The developing countries suffer from the illusion of sustainable development under globalisation regime.

13.1. NEWTONIAN PARADIGM

The dominating paradigm of our time is the Newtonian, mechanistic model which emphasizes reductionism and separatism, the separation of mind and matter, and postulates the existence of an objective universe outside of us. It permeates every aspect of society. This has been a very successful paradigm in that it has been the driving force in bringing about the tremendous advances in our material well-being over the last three centuries. It is no coincidence that Western society is materialistic, consumption-oriented, and spiritually barren. These are all direct consequences of the Newtonian paradigm. The great majority of our citizens take these values as obvious and natural, but in the larger picture of civilizations, they are not. They are quite subjective. Things are interconnected, but in ways that we do not yet understand. Environmental crisis is a direct consequence of the very effective mechanical paradigm running its course. One could say that the seeds of its destruction were built into its very success. The current crisis is a problem of scale more than anything else. The strategy of exploiting natural resources for the benefit of mankind using reductionist science was quite appropriate when the population was relatively small and the environmental impact was limited, but became disastrous when continued on a fully populated planet with an advanced technology. It would have been absurd to introduce environmental protection in the early days of the industrial revolution. However today, the population is enormous. There are no new frontiers to move into like in the good old days. We have now discovered that we live on a finite planet.

13.2. THE LPG MODEL

Globalisation has the noble intention of international integration and interdependence. It is very logical . It has substantial core of truth. It is embedded in free market policy which ensure efficiency through competition. Globalization" claims that it can deliver optimal resource allocation by removing the barriers to "free trade". Furthermore it promises sustainable growth, increased employment and a higher standard of living. But "the LPG model of Global integration" is not only based on a faulty theoretical foundation, and very unlikely to deliver sustainable growth. Moving very fast in the economic ladder does not mean much unless it is sustainable. In neoclassical economics, the efficient allocation of resources depends on the counting and internalization of all costs. But costs in the modern world are not internalized. The result is that we get a distorted use of resources that rewards those who exploit the situation by producing the wrong things at the wrong prices and are able to pass on the real costs of running their businesses to the general public . The "free trade system" could more tellingly be called the "free ride system", because TNC's do not have to include in their product costs all the indirect costs they cause society, such as pollution of the land, sea and air, ozone holes, disappearing topsoil, exploding health costs, allergies, global warming, destruction of species, pesticides in food, antibiotic-resistant bacteria, crime, unemployment, escalating social costs, etc. Many of the most common, and most damaging products on the market, would never be manufactured if they were priced at their real costs to society as a whole. The road to success in global business today is to find a way to pass on as many of your costs as possible to the public, preferably to another country's public. The most profitable companies at this time are those that are most successful at getting someone else to pay the real costs of their doing business. Another fundamental axiom in Operations Research, which is valid for any optimization problem, is that proper resource allocation requires that benefits and costs must accrue to the same decision maker. Otherwise, you get distortion, i.e. the wrong solution, from a total point of view. And this kind of distortion is precisely what happens with the TNC's because of the failure to internalize costs. A corporation has many so-called "stakeholders" - i.e. people who have an intrinsic interest in the decisions. However, "globalization" maximizes only the profits to the shareholders, while all the other stakeholders are left bearing the costs, for example, cleaning up the environment and dealing with unemployment when the corporation decides to move on to a more attractive(i.e. cheaper) location.

FDI fell to generate backward linkages that help developing countries to develop, and in many cases wiped out locally competing firms thereby "crowding out" domestic investment. The Working Group found that investment regime liberalization-led FDI has had at best a limited success in all developing countries. According to them FDI is not an end but a means to sustainable development. Simply attracting FDI is not enough to generate economic growth in an environmentally sustainable manner. Even in the nations that received the lion's share of FDI in the region— Brazil, Argentina, and Mexico—FDI fell short of generating spillovers and sustained economic growth. FDI needs to be part of a comprehensive development strategy aimed at raising the standards of living of the nation's population with minimal damage to the environment. FDI policy needs to be conducted in parallel with significant and targeted domestic policies that upgrade the capabilities of national firms and provide a benchmark of environmental protection.

International agreements, whether at the WTO or at the level of regional or bi-lateral trade and/or investment treaties (RBTIAs), need to leave developing nations the "policy space" to pursue the domestic policies necessary to foster sustainable development through FDI. Thus new directions for FDI is needed for achieving sustainable development. Hence, it is imperative to rethink about the role of FDI in the developing economies.

Free market does not necessarily remain fair. Instead of 'pro-market strategy' we adopt 'pro-business strategy'. Privatisation process through pro-marketism is not bad but commercialization, though pro-businessism of every thing is bad . Profit is not bad but profiteering is bad.. So while later type globalization process in India maximizes the benefits to shareholders, and penalizes the other stakeholders, it is by no means clear whether there is any positive benefit at all in "free ride markets" to society as a whole. Indeed, there are indications that the marginal costs to the environment alone now exceed any benefits to the shareholders. Thus "globalization" should rightly be called Shareholder Protectionism, since that is really what it is all about. Unfortunately, both the public, and our politicians, have, under the powerful influence of the business sector, taken globalization on board as their agenda for our common future.

13.3. CONCLUDING REMARKS:

The sustainable development has three interdependent and mutually reinforcing pillars: economic development, social development, and environmental protection. It does not focus solely on environmental issues. We should differentiate betgween green development and sustainable development . The proponents of green development prioritizes environmental sustainability over economic and cultural considerations. But cultural diversity is as necessary for humankind as biodiversity is for nature. It is one of the roots of development understood not simply in terms of economic growth, but also as a means to achieve a more satisfactory intellectual, emotional, moral and spiritual existence. In this sense, cultural diversity is the fourth policy area of sustainable development. Developing countries are not only rich in biodiversity but also in cultural diversity.

Thus the problem of north and south are to be perceived separately. Many scholars do not like to disaggregate the issue since they think that such analysis is unnecessarily divisive. But the aggregative view of the problem of the world is non-social and highly concealing. It aims at ensuring individual success at the cost social welfare. Micro success coexists with but macro failure. To concentrate on problem of the modernity without focusing on developing countries can be misleading in terms of causation and consequences. Therefore such classification is very meaningful for developing countries. The emerging commercialization process in India seems to be less compatible for social development and for the sustainability of economic development process of India. We should examine the growth sustainability of different sectors like health , education, agriculture, tourism and industry of developing countries in dynamics and environmental aspects that form the sustainability issue because our country encounters the dual objective of economic development and environmental conservation. For having sustainable development for India in the new millennium we should build an economy through a decentralised model of community participation which will initiate a sustainable process of green development , which warrants a sound infrastructural base through a proactive public policy. We have to redefine the role of the state the long run and short run. We should make insightful study which should capture the social which should not depend on fragmented policy any more. It should reemphasise on future but not the present, conservation but not the consumption, protection but not the production. Market can not solve the very problem that it creates. There is fear that the current economic crisis might overshadow environmental concerns. Costs of inaction on key Environmental Challenges, not responding adequately to these challenges can be very dangerous. Otherwise sustainable development will be a set of wishful characteristics of a future society.

There are two groups of economist having two different views on sustainable development. One group is very pessimistic. They focus on heavy population pressure and overexploitation of natural resources. They caution us regarding the degeneration of the carrying capacity of the spacecraft. They believe that we are heading towards a disastrous situation. Other group is very optimistic. They claim that science always discovers the alternatives. Market always produces the efficient technology which minimizes the use of scarce resources. But we can not be pessimistic nor can we afford to be optimistic. We have to be realistic. We should not be pessimistic and afraid of the contradictions within the various ideas that make up sustainable development. We have to wake up. We should recognize the dangers of an overgovernance and over commitment of public sector and over exploitation of resources by the private sector.

Thus in order to achieve sustainable development two sets of policies are warranted:

A) *Harnessing Positive Links by:*

Stoping excessive resource use

Clarifying Property Rights

B) *Breaking the Negative Links by:*

Tradeoff should be identified

Cost benefit of alternative policies should be assessed

Priorities/standards should be set

Practical cost effective policies should be designed to force change in behaviour

These are possible by :

i) Improving information base

ii) Changing Institutional Setup

iii) Involving/empowering local People

There are many contradictions and inconsistencies. It poses a great dilemma and great challenge. Confronting the challenge is very costly but not facing the challenge is really disastrous for the whole society. Therefore the idea of sustainable development should be less idealistic and more practical. The Sustainable development should reconcile the 'need to produce' and the 'need to protect'. At theoretical level there is large agreements but at practical level there is large gaps. Therefore we need to outline a series of "strategic imperatives," or "critical objectives," inherent in the concept of sustainable development. These include: reviving growth; changing the quality of growth; meeting essential needs for jobs, food, energy, water, and sanitation; ensuring a sustainable level of population; conserving and enhancing the resource base; reorienting technology and managing risk; and merging environment and economics in decision making . If we keep our heads, recognize the seriousness of the environmental crisis, and then act boldly to meet the various challenges of that crisis, we can not only turn around the quality of the environment, but we can keep a vibrant economy as well. We do not have to choose between an environmentally healthy and economically robust nation. Both are compatible. We can have both. We are intelligent enough, have the ability to develop enough new technologies, and can change our behaviors enough to confront all the problems facing us and create the optimal solutions. Thus, development, in the context of sustainable development, means that the developing economies will become equal to the developed world's economies. This, in turn, will alleviate poverty and suffering in poor countries and make the world more equitable for all human beings. Poor men and women of developing countries depend heavily on natural resources for their livelihoods and food security, but suffer from inadequate access and declining quality of these environmental assets. So we should give adequate priority to the role of improved environmental management, in order to achieve the Millennium Development Goals (MDGs). Technology and innovation play a key role in sustainable development. However, our socio-economic system does not provide adequate drivers of innovation and technological change aimed at this goal. We should, therefore explore how innovation and technology can better contribute to sustainable development. The State should create conditions which encourage the people to save the environment.

Bibliography

Ahluwalia, I J (1991) Productivity and Growth in Indina Manufacturing , Oxford Univ.Press Delhi

Appenzeller, Tim, "Environment and the Economy," *Science*, Vol. 260, June 1993,

Barbier, E.B. (1989), *Economics, Natural Resources Scarcity and Development,* Earth Scan, London.

Barkley, P W and DW Seckler, Economic Growth and Environmental Decay, Harcourt Brace, New York, 1972

Baumol, W J and W E Oates, The Theory of Environmental Policy, Prentice hall, Englewood Cliffs, 1975

Berkes, F.(1985) The Common Property Resources problem and the creation of limited property rights, *The Human Ecology,* Vo113:187-208.

Bhagwati, J (1993) India in Transition: Freeing the Economy: Oxford ClarendonPress Chandrasekhar, S(1995), Technology Priorities for India's Development: need for restructuring , *Economic Political Weekly*, Oct 28

Borelli, Peter (1988), *Cross Roads: Environmental Priorities for the Future,* Island Press.

Brown, L.R. (1981), *Building a Sustainable Society,* W.W. Norton, New York.

Brown, L.R., et at. (1993), *The State of the World,* Report of the World Watch Institute on Progress towards a Sustainable Society, New York.

Bruno, Clémentin et Vincent Cheynet, Contre le developpement durable

Buchanan, J M and WC Stubblebine, Externality, Economics, Vol.29, (pp.371-84), 1962

Carley, Michael and Christie, Ian, Managing Sustainable Development (Minneapolis: University of Minnesota Press, 1993).

Cohen, B. & Winn, M. I. 2007. Market imperfections, opportunity and sustainable entrepreneurship. Journal of Business Venturing, 22(1): 29-49.

Daly, H. E. 1973. Towards a Steady State Economy. San Francisco: Freeman. Daly, H. E. 1991. Steady-State Economics (2nd ed.). Washington, D.C.: Island Press.

Das, Kumar (1988), Ecosystem Approach, *Indian journal of Regional Science,* Vol. XX(1)

Das, Kumar(1990) Intergenerational Approach for Sustainable Development, Proceedings of 11th International Seminar on Environmental Impact Assessment, held at University of Aberdeen, August

Das, Kumar, (1990), *Energy and Rural Economic Development* in *India,* Ashish, Delhi.

Das, Kumar, (1993), *Environment and Development Conundrum,* Discovery Publishing House, New Delhi (ed.)

Das, Kumar, (1994), Environmental Impact of Industrialisation in Eastern Ghat, Ministry of Environment and Forest, Govt. of India, Delhi.

DeSimone, L. & Popoff, F. 1997. Eco-efficiency: The business link to sustainable development. Cambridge: MIT Press.

Donella H. Meadows, it. al- (1972) The *Limits to growth* Universe Books for Polomal Associates, New York.

Dovers, Stephen R. and Handmer, John W., "Contradictions

in Sustainability," *Environmental Conservation*, Vol. 20., No. 3, Autumn 1993, pp. 217 - 222.

Dyllick, T. & Hockerts, K. 2002. Beyond the business case for corporate sustainability. Business Strategy and the Environment, 11(2): 130-141

Edel, M, Economics and the Environment, Prentice hall, Englewoods Cliffs, 1973

Freeman, A M et al Economics of Environmental Policy, Wiley, New York, 1973

Friedman, Milton and Friedman, Rose, Free To Choose ,New York: Avon Books, 1979.

Goldsmith, E. et al. (1988), *The Earth Report: The guide to global Ecological Issues,* Princeton Sloan.

Gupta, S P (2006)Globalisation, Economic Reforms and Employment Strategy in India, **Academic Foundation, Delhi** , 276 P

Haas, Peter M.; Levy, Marc A.; Parson, Edward A., "The Earth Summit, How Should We Judge UNCED's Success?" *Environment*, Vol. 34, No. 8, October 1992, pp. 7 - 32.

Hasna, A. M. (2007). "Dimensions of sustainability". *Journal of Engineering for Sustainable Development: Energy, Environment, and Health* **2** (1): 47–57.

Hanumantha Rao, C , B B Bhattacharya , N S Siddharthan (2005) Indian Economy and Society in the Era of Globalisation , **Academic Foundation, Delhi,** 439p

Hashim,S R (1998) Economic Growth and Income Distribution, *Economic and Political Weekly,* March 21-27

Hekstra, G.P. (1989), Global Warning and Rising Sea Levels, *The Ecologists,* Vol. 19(1)

Herfindahl, OC and AV Kneese, Economic Theory of Natural resources, Merrill Pub. Co, Columbus, 1974 Maler, KG

Environmental Economics, John Hopkins Press, Baltimore, 1974

Hussain, M. (1994), *Sustainable Development,* RRH Publishing, New Delhi (ed).

Jean-marc, A quoi sert le développement durable ? décembre 2002, site de l'auteur : www.manicore.com - contacter l'auteur : jean-marc@manicore.com

Jodha, N S.(1986) Common property resources and the rural Poor in dry regions of India, *Economic and Political Weekly* ,21 July 5: 1169-81

John,Baden, L'économie politique du développement durable, document de l'ICREI Foundation fro Rseasrch on Economics and the Envirponment (FREE),1997

Kapila , Raj & Uma Kapila (1996) **Understanding India's Economic Reforms , Academic Foundation, Delhi**

Krueger, Anne O (2002) Economic Policy Reforms and the Indian Economy(ed) , University of Chicago Press

Kainath, G S.(1992) Strategy for development of Marine Fishery, *Financial Express* ,4th Jan.

Kothan, R. (1982), *Environment and Development in Asia and the Pacific Experiences and Prospects,* UNEP.

Luc Ferry, Protéger l'espèce humaine contre elle-même », entretien avec dans la *Revue des Deux Mondes*, octobre-novembre 2007, pp.75-79

Marchand, J M and KP Russell, Externality, Liability, Separability and resource Allocation, American economics review, Vol. 63, pp. 611-20, 1975

Meade, J E, The Theory of Economic Externalities, Sijthoff, Leiden, 1973

Mishan, E J, The Costs of Economic Growth, Staples press, London, 1968

Meadows, D., Meadows, D. L., Randers, J., & Behrens, W. 1971. The Limits to Growth. New York: Universe

Books.

Meadows, D.H., et al. (1972), *The Limits to Growth,* Signet, New York.

Mehta , Pradeep S (2006) A Functional Competition Policy For India, **Academic Foundation, Delhi** ,294p

Milbrath, Lester, W., Envisioning a Sustainable Society, Learning Our Way Out ,New York: State University of New York Press, 1989.

Mitra , A (1999) Total Factor Productivity and Technical Efficiency in Indian Industries, Economic and Political weekly, July 31

Murphy, E. P. (1967) *Governing Nature,* Quadrangle Books, Chicago.

Nagaraj , R(2006)Aspects of India's Economic Growth and Reforms, **Academic Foundation, Delhi** ,352p

Nayyar, Deepak(ed) (1997) *Industrial Growth and Stagnation*, Oxford University Press, New Delhi

National Commission on the Environment, "Choosing a Sustainable Future," Washington DC: Island Press, 1993.

Nijkamp, P, et al. (1993), *Dynamic Modeling for Sustainable Development,* Revue European Des Sociales Science, Vol. XXXI (96).

Odum, E. P. (1976) The strategy of Ecosystem development in the *Ecology of Man* (ed) Robert Leo Smith, Section-III, Harper and Row.

Partnership for the decades of Education for Sustainable Development Retrieved on: 2007-07-16

Pearce, P.W. and Atkinson, G. (1992), *Measuring Sustainable Development,* CRERGE University College of London.

Radhakrishna, R. S.K. Rao, S. Mahendra Dev and K. Subbarao (2006) India in a Globalising World, **Academic Foundation, Delhi** , 528p

Rodrik, Dani (2000). 'How Far Will International Economic Integration go?' *Journal of Economic Perspectives*, 14/ 4: 177-186.

Rangaranjan C (2002) Economic Reforms: Some issues and Concerns, The Indina Economic Journal, Vol.49(2) Dec.

Redclift, M. (1987), *Sustainable Development,* Methuen, London

Report of World Summit on Sustainable Development, WSSD 2002 , Johannesburg, South Africa, 26 Aug-4 Sept 2002.

Ridkar, R. K. (1973) To grow or Not to grow-thats not the Relevant Question, *Science,* 182 pp. 1315-18.

Robertson, James, Future Wealth, A New Economics for the 21st Century ,New York: The Bootstrap Press, 1990.

Sam, H. Schurr (1972), *Energy, Economic Growth and the Environment,* John Hopkins University Press (ed).

Schaltegger, S. & Sturm, A. 1998. Eco-Efficiency by Eco-Controlling. Zürich: vdf.

Schneider, S.H. (1989), *Global Warming: Are we entering the Green House Country,* Sierra Club, Boon.

Singh, Kartar (1993) Marine Fishermen Cooperatives in Kerala, Working paper *No.40, Anand, Institute of Rural Management.*

Smith, R. L. (1976) (ed). The *Ecology of Man* an *Ecosystem* Approach, Harpar & Row.

Smith, R.I. (1976), *The Ecology of Man,* Harper and Row, London (ed).

Smith, W.R. (1982), *Energy from Forest Biomass,* Academic Press, New York (ed).

Srivastav, UK and Dharma Reddy (1983), *Fishery Development in India,* Concept Pub, New Delhi

Stivers, R. 1976. The Sustainable Society: Ethics and Economic Growth. Philadelphia: Westminster Press.

Sutinen, jon g. Major challenges for fishery policy reform: A political economy perspective , university of rhode island ,OECD trade and agriculturc, working paper 2008/8

Sylvie, Brunel sur, Les enjeux internationaux », entretien avec France Culture, 11 juin 2008

Temple, Stanley, interview remarks, "Old Issue, New Urgency?" *Wisconsin Environmental Dimension*, Spring 1992, Vol. 1, No. 1

Tobla, M.K. (1984), *Sustainable Development,* Butterworths, London.

United Nations Division for sustainable Development. Documents: Sustainable Development Issues Retrieved: 2007 05-12

United Nations. 1987."Report of the World Commission on Environmcnt and Development." General Assembly Resolution 42/187, 11 December 1987. Retrieved: 2007-04-12

US Partnership for the Decade of Education for Sustainable Development. Retrieved on: 2007-07-16

Vandana, Shiva and J. Bandopadhyay (1988), Political Economy of Ecology Movements, *Economic*

and Political Weekly, Vol. XXIII (4), June.

Vandana, Shiva, *Stolen Harvest* ,South End Press, 2000, pp 61–62:

Vaidyanathan, A (2003) India's Economic Reforms and Development, **Academic Foundation, Delhi**

Virmani ,Arvind (2006) Propelling India from Socialist Stagnation to Global Power , **Academic Foundation, Delhi**

Victor,PA, Economics of Pollution, Mac Millan, London, 1972

WCED, (1987), *Our Common Future,* Oxford Univ. Press, Oxford.

WHO, 2005 World Summit Outcome Document, World Health Organization, 15 September 2005

Will, Allen. 2007."Learning for Sustainability: Sustainable Development."

Wolozin, H (ed) The Economics of Pollution, General Learning Press, Morristown, 1974

Working Group on Development and the Environment in the Americas, *Globalization and the Environment: Lessons from the Americas*, Heinrich Böll Foundation North America, Washington, May 2008

World Commission on Environment and Development, Our Common Future ,Oxford, England: Oxford University Press, 1988.